Homeowner's Rights

A Legal Guide to Your Neighborhood

Other books in the *Rights* series:

Attorney Responsibilities & Client Rights
by Suzan Herskowitz Singer

Employees' Rights
by Richard C. Busse

Employer's Rights
by Charles H. Fleischer

Gay & Lesbian Rights
by Brette McWhorter Sember

Teen Rights
by Traci Truly

Traveler's Rights
by Alexander Anolik and John K. Hawks

Unmarried Parents' Rights, 2nd Ed.
by Jacqueline D. Stanley

Homeowner's Rights

A Legal Guide to Your Neighborhood

Mark Warda
Attorney at Law

SPHINX® PUBLISHING
AN IMPRINT OF SOURCEBOOKS, INC.®
NAPERVILLE, ILLINOIS
www.SphinxLegal.com

1-04 19.95

First Edition, 2004

Published by: Sphinx® Publishing, An Imprint of Sourcebooks, Inc.®

Naperville Office
P.O. Box 4410
Naperville, Illinois 60567-4410
630-961-3900
Fax: 630-961-2168
www.sourcebooks.com
www.SphinxLegal.com

This publication is designed to provide accurate and authoritative information in
regard to the subject matter covered. It is sold with the understanding that the pub-
lisher is not engaged in rendering legal, accounting, or other professional service. If
legal advice or other expert assistance is required, the services of a competent professional person should be sought.
*From a Declaration of Principles Jointly Adopted by a Committee of the
American Bar Association and a Committee of Publishers and Associations*

This product is not a substitute for legal advice.
Disclaimer required by Texas statutes.

Library of Congress Cataloging-in-Publication Data
Warda, Mark.
  Homeowner's rights : a legal guide to your neighborhood / by Mark
Warda.-- 1st ed.
    p. cm.
  ISBN 1-57248-334-2 (alk. paper)
  1. Homeowners--Legal status, laws, etc.--United States. 2. Home
ownership--Law and legislation--United States--Popular works. 3.
Homeowners--United States--Handbooks, manuals, etc. I. Title.

KF390.H53 W37 2004
346.7304'32--dc22
                                          2004025214

Printed and bound in the United States of America.

BG Paperback — 10 9 8 7 6 5 4 3 2 1

DEDICATION

I dedicate this book to my wife, Alexandra,
who left her family and her county
to share her life with me.

CONTENTS

INTRODUCTION

Peoples' homes are supposed to be their castles, but when one neighbor is bouncing a basketball outside your bedroom window and another is filling your house with smoke from burning trash, it doesn't seem that way. When the peace and solitude of our home life are disturbed by sounds or smells, or our property itself is invaded by people, animals, plants or debris from our neighbors we naturally get upset. If we can't stop it we may get incensed.

With more people living in less space and lot sizes getting smaller, we are affected by our neighbors more than ever. Often the disagreements can be worked out calmly, but sometimes they seem irreconcilable. When we can't work out a problem directly with a neighbor, we must resort to the legal system to settle our differences. This book explains how to use that system to solve neighbor disputes.

Besides neighbors, government employees can assault our castles. They can build airports and prisons next door, fine us for cutting down our own trees or changing our building without permission, and stop us from trying to earn a living from our living room. Your rights and remedies when dealing with government agents are also explained in this book.

Other claims against our property can come from companies that do work for us or run utilities in our neighborhood. Workers can have a court sell your house if you do not pay. Utilities may use your property for their lines unless you know your rights guaranteed by the Supreme Court and your subdivision restrictions.

While the title of this book is *Homeowner's Rights*, most of the principles in this book apply to renters as well. In most cases, a tenant has the same rights and obligations as an owner. The difference is that the tenant has the rights for a fixed time.

Some of the examples in this book are very recent, but others are very old. The same problems between neighbors have come up again and again over the centuries, so many of the legal principles of neighbor law are well settled. In researching nuisances and trespass, two of the most common areas of neighbor law, it is not unusual to find very similar problems in cases a hundred years old. Dig a little deeper and you will find a similar case from two hundred or three hundred years ago. As for trespass cases, these are among the oldest cases for which written records exist!

This book is written in the hope that if people can learn their legal rights and responsibilities, they can avoid spending their money and a court's time fighting over them. Considering the cost of going to court, this book can save you hundreds or thousands of dollars if it helps you settle your differences yourself.

However, when reading the cases in this book, it must be kept in mind that each case has a unique set of facts and each state has its own set of laws and court opinions. Every rule of law has exceptions and seemingly small differences in your case can make a big difference in the result as compared to an example in this book. The importance of the cases in this book is to show you how a court looks at these types of cases. That way, you won't have to waste a lot of time and money if you know your position is weak.

Courts seem to have fun with silly neighbor dispute cases. In ruling on a tree case a court might talk about the "root" of the issue, and then go on to analyze the state of "tree law" across the entire country. In a cat case, a state supreme court justice might mention some good books on the history of cats. A surprising number of the cases have been appealed as high as the supreme courts of the various states.

Many of the sections in this book can be the subject of entire books. It is therefore impossible to cover every aspect of each area of neighbor law in a book like this. The intent of this book is to give you the basic principles in each area law related to ownership of your home or condo. For further information on any subject of particular interest, the last section of this book explains legal research. In most instances, there is much more detailed information readily available.

The first chapter of this book explains the laws and regulations that affect your rights as a homeowner. Chapter 2 discusses potential issues relating to property and zoning. Chapter 3 instructs the reader regarding nuisances. Problems that can occur with property boundaries are explained in Chapter 4. Water rights and other environmental situations are described in Chapter 5. Chapter 6 explains ways to avoid a dispute with your neighbors. Chapter 7 explains the best ways to win a dispute with your neighbor if you are not able to settle it. Chapter 8 explains how to handle challenges with government agencies such as building departments and zoning boards. If all else fails, Chapter 9 explains, in detail, how to go to court over a neighbor dispute. Finally, Chapter 10 explains how to do legal research to find out more about your rights in a specific situation.

–1–
LEARNING YOUR RIGHTS

Before you begin to tackle a problem regarding rights to your property, you need to know your legal rights. It could be that expectations of your rights is exaggerated and your neighbor will win. Perhaps your best tact is to bluff or to concede something in the case. If you know exactly what your rights are to begin with, you can plan your approach accordingly.

There are two sides to every dispute and while each side usually fervently believes he or she is right and is being wronged, no more than fifty percent of all neighbors fighting about something are right. In fact, a lot less than fifty percent are right because the law is rarely black and white and most homeowners expect their rights are greater than they are.

Consider one neighbor whose daughter practices the piano each afternoon and another who needs to sleep in the afternoon. The child's mother thinks the other is an unreasonable, old, child-hating grouch. The other thinks the mother is a child-spoiling inconsiderate tormenter. Who's right? It all depends on where they live and which rules or laws apply.

Your legal rights as a homeowner (or renter) are determined by many factors. Depending on where you live, there may be private rules and regulations on your property, city or county ordinances, zoning laws and regulations, state statutes, federal laws, state or federal constitutional rights, and general common law principles that give you and your neighbor rights.

DEVELOPMENT RULES AND RESTRICTIVE COVENANTS

Development rules and *restrictive covenants* are sets of rules governing the use of property that are voluntarily put on the property by the owners. These may be basic *restrictions* that say that only *single-family homes* may be built on the lots, or they may be elaborate rules that even control what color the homes may be painted and what color the curtains may be. Restrictive covenants may be in the form of *deed restrictions*, a *condominium declaration*, or other similar legal document.

You may wonder why a person would put a restriction on his own property stating what color he may paint his house or what he can build on the land. These restrictions are usually put on the property by *developers* who turn raw land into subdivisions. The restrictions make the lots more valuable because they insure that the character of the neighborhood will remain the same. Controlling the use of all lots in a subdivision protects the owners from those things that could devalue their properties.

> **Example:** Consider a large executive home in an area where only single-family homes can be built and where lots must be at least five acres. How would the value of a home be affected if someone could put several mobile homes or a used car business on the lot next door?

General Restrictions

There are hundreds of types of restrictions placed on property. The most common of them allow only single-family homes to be built. Other restrictions say no clotheslines may be set up in the front yard; boats may not be stored on the property; or, that the building must be a certain size and must be set back a certain distance from the street.

Years ago it was common to put restrictions on property that it could "not be sold to anyone not of the Caucasian race" or similar language. However, these restrictions have been held null and void by the United States Supreme Court.

Occasionally an article will appear in the newspaper that will describe someone at war with his neighbors because he wants to do something in violation of one of these restrictions. Often it will seem like an innocent thing the person wants to do, like paint his house a color forbidden in the restrictions or put up a basketball hoop for his kids. The person will be outraged that a court is telling him what to do with his *own* property. He will scream that this is no longer a free country.

However, in cases based upon property restrictions like these, the court is not enforcing the government's will against people. It is enforcing a *contract* between citizens—restrictions voluntarily placed on property by its original owner. Every person buying a piece of property should know what they are buying and what restrictions have been placed on it. By accepting a *deed* to a piece of property, a person agrees to abide by the restrictions that are on it. Therefore, he cannot complain when they are enforced.

Unfortunately, few people read the restrictions before buying property and fewer understand them. The picket fence is so cute and the kitchen so clean that they sign the contract without a thought. They don't stop to think that they might not be able to keep their boat or their truck on the property, or raise dogs in the yard. *Real estate agents* aren't eager to disclose restrictions since they may kill the deal. *Title companies* usually do not have the restrictions ready to show the buyer until the day of closing. Many people, in some areas at least, do not choose to have an attorney represent them in the purchase of their home.

A *real estate contract* should not be signed until the buyer has read all of the restrictions (and *zoning laws*) affecting the property. At minimum, there should be a clause in the contract making the sale contingent upon buyer determining that the restrictions do not affect his use of the property.

To find out if there are restrictions on your property or your neighbor's property, check the papers you received when purchasing your property and the county recorder's office at your city hall or county courthouse.

Subdivisions

If you received either a *title insurance policy* or an *abstract of title* when you purchased your property, it should list the restrictions that apply to your property. Usually they were put on the property around the time that the land was *subdivided* into lots.

Sometimes there are two or more sets of restrictions placed on property. Also, keep in mind that although two pieces of property are next to each other, they may be in different subdivisions and therefore subject to different restrictions—check both your property and your neighbor's. If you and your troublesome neighbor are in different subdivisions, you may not be able to do anything to enforce the restrictions on his property. (One of his other neighbors would have to do it.)

If your property is not in a *platted subdivision*, it may not have any restrictions on it. If it does have restrictions, they would usually be contained in the deed. If they have once been put in a deed, they should have been repeated in every deed of the same property executed in the future.

You can usually tell whether your property is subdivided by checking the legal description on your deed. If your property is described as a certain lot by number, it is in a subdivision. If it is described by a long description such as "Starting at the northwest corner...run East 55 feet...etc.," then it is probably land that has never been subdivided.

If your property is a *condominium, planned unit development (PUD)* or similar development, there will be restrictions, rules, and regulations filed with the original development of the property. Sometimes these run hundreds of pages. You should have received a copy when you bought your unit. If not, you should be able to get a copy from the *management company* or the *board or directors*. (If they ask a ridiculous price for a copy, you can view a copy for free in the public records office and possibly make copies of just the pages you need. There may also be a provision on the rules or in your state law limiting the amount that can be charged for a copy.)

There may also be rules and regulations that are not filed in the public records. For example, in a mobile home park, they may be posted somewhere on the property or given to the residents. In some cases there cannot be such unrecorded rules unless the recorded rules say there can. But where lots are rented, the leases may allow for additional rules. Read the recorded rules carefully and ask the management company or board of directors for copies of any such rules.

Recorder's Restrictions

If you cannot find out what restrictions affect your property or your neighbor's property, check with the recorder's office, a title company, or an attorney. Some recorder's offices keep a separate listing of restrictions that is easy to use, but others have complicated systems that are difficult. If you cannot find the information at the courthouse, check with a title company or attorney who specializes in real estate law.

If you do not know to whom to go, you might check with a friend who is in the real estate business. He or she would probably know who can provide the service at a reasonable price. With something like this, it pays to compare prices. One attorney or title company might be able to provide the information for $25 or less, while another might charge several hundred dollars for the same information.

If it is found that an annoyance in the neighborhood violates restrictions on the property—there is a *remedy*. The bad news is that it may involve an expensive court action. The good news is that several of the neighbors may join together and split the cost. In some cases, a letter from an attorney is enough to solve the problem. If the offending party is clearly in the wrong, he will be told so by his own attorney. When he realizes the potential cost of continuing the violation, he will likely stop.

Keep in mind that it is possible, even if your neighbor is right next door, that his restrictions will be different from yours. Compare the legal description of his property with that of yours. Be sure you know which restrictions apply to his.

However, if the issue is fuzzy, such as if the wording is not clear enough to cover the activity or if other violations have been allowed in the past, then the party may decide to ignore the restriction. In such a case, the remedy is a court action for an *injunction*. This is an action where you ask a judge to *enjoin the activity*, meaning to order that it be stopped. If it is not stopped, the person can be fined or jailed.

Such a suit is usually expensive. In most cases, it is impossible without the services of an attorney. The restrictions will often say that the violator will have to pay the attorney's fees of the persons enforcing the restrictions. However, he or she may win and the persons attempting to enforce the restrictions will have to pay *his or her* attorney's fees.

CONDOMINIUM RULES

Life in *condominium* developments is controlled by five sets of rules:

- ◆ constitutional rights;
- ◆ specific laws;
- ◆ zoning laws;
- ◆ property restrictions; and,
- ◆ common law principles.

The specific laws are usually contained in the state *Condominium Act*. This is the law that controls the division of property into condominiums. The property restrictions are usually contained in the *Declaration of Condominium* creating the condominium and also the *bylaws* and other rules and regulations adopted by the individual condominium. Where the rights of the parties are not spelled-out in the statute or condominium documents, then common law principles are used by judges to make decisions.

(An explanation of all the details of condominium law is beyond the scope of this book. However, the legal principles that apply to people in condominiums and the ways to research those principles are the same.)

If you have a problem with your neighbor in a condominium, you should first check all of the rules governing the condominium. These would include the *Declaration of Condominium* and all amendments to it, the bylaws of the association that runs the condominium and all amendments to them, and any rules or regulations established by the *condominium association*.

You should have gotten some of these documents when you bought or rented your unit. If not, you should be able to get them from the association. In most states you have a clear *right of access* to these documents at all reasonable times. Be sure to ask to see all *amendments*. (You may be able to see the declaration and its amendments and some restrictions in the records department of the courthouse; the bylaws will probably not be recorded there.)

If the answer to your problem is not found in these documents, or if your problem is *caused* by these documents, check your state condominium act. You can usually find it at your local library or you may be able to obtain a copy from your state legislator (not your congressman or U.S. senator) or from your state capitol. If you check your state's condominium laws, you may find that your association is not following them or has passed some rule in violation of the state law. Keep in mind, though, that laws are not always interpreted to mean what they seem to say. The explanation of a law may be ten times as long as a law. To find out more about what the condominium laws mean, go to a law library at a courthouse or at a law school. (Chapter 10 in this book explains how to get started in researching the law.)

Zoning Laws

Zoning laws also cover condominium developments, but it is unlikely that a matter covered by zoning would not be covered by an even stricter rule in the condominium act or restrictions.

> **Example:** A person is operating a business out of his condo-
> minium in violation of zoning laws, it is probably also
> against the condominium restrictions. However, it
> may be easier to stop someone by calling a *zoning
> inspector* than waiting for the *condominium board* to
> take action.

If there is nothing in the statutes or rules covering the situation,
some relief may be found in the common law principles regarding
nuisance, trespass, and other matters discussed later in this chapter.

🏠 *After a couple received consent from the developer of
their condominium to install marble tile in their unit in the
Harrison Heights complex in Munster, Indiana, their
downstairs neighbor was unable to sleep due to the
"clicking, clacking, clapping, tapping, scraping, rumbling,
and thumping" coming form their unit. He said it sounded
like "barrels rolling, someone dropping lead buckshot,
furniture-moving, wheels rolling, heavy objects hitting the
floor, and all manner of walking noises from both soft and
hard shoes. The condominium association first ordered
the couple to carpet the unit, but later changed their mind
based upon the oral consent of the developer. The couple
told the downstairs neighbor that if he didn't like the noise
he could move. He tried to sell his unit, but when a
prospective purchaser heard the noise he did not come
back. He sued and was awarded $5,000, but not his attor-
neys fees.*

ZONING LAWS

Laws defining what can be done on property in certain designated
areas are called *zoning laws* or *zoning ordinances.* A typical zoning
ordinance will divide a city or county into separate districts such as
residential, office, commercial, industrial, or agricultural. Some ordinances will have sub-classifications such as R-1, R-2, R-3 for

residential, where different types of residential uses are allowed in each district. One district may allow only single-family homes on at least three-acre lots and another may allow up to twenty units per acre.

Zoning laws not only define what use may be made of a piece of property, they also may define how that property may be used within that classification.

A zoning law may define how many stories a home may be, how big a garage may be, and even what constitutes a single family.

> **Example 1:** Two unrelated students rent a house in a single-family district. Do they violate the single-family rule? What if they are engaged to be married or are sleeping in one bed? What if they are brother and sister sleeping in separate rooms? What if they are two unrelated men sleeping in the same bed?

> **Example 2:** Suppose that next door to the two students live a couple, their four children (one of whom has her own baby) and two of the couple's parents. Are they a single family? If so, does it make sense for the law to allow nine people in one house, but to forbid two students in the house next door? What if the family is in a cult and the students are scholars?

As you can see, zoning laws (like most laws) can present some difficult questions. The answers to these questions can only be answered by looking at the exact wording of the zoning law, any other state or local laws on the matter, how they are interpreted by the courts and how the courts interpret the state and federal constitutions. (In the above examples, some courts have held that distinctions between married and unmarried couples violates the equal protection clauses of the constitution.)

To find out if your neighbors' behavior violates a zoning ordinance, check with the local zoning department. This may be part of the county or city or it may be that both governments have zoning ordinances that overlap. If you discuss your neighbor problem with someone at the zoning department, he or she may be able to take action to eliminate the problem. If the person you talk to says that the activity is not illegal or that nothing can be done, do not take them at their word. Ask someone else in the department or research the matter yourself.

Usually a governmental regulation, such as zoning, must be enforced by government action. But in some areas, private parties have a right to enforce zoning laws. This right may be given by state statute, local ordinance, or by court decisions.

Two types of court actions may be brought to enforce zoning laws. One is an action for an injunction against the violator and the other is a request for a *writ of mandamus* against the zoning department. A writ of mandamus is a court order requiring a public official to perform some duty. Requests for both an injunction and a writ of mandamus may sometimes be included in the same suit.

However, not all areas of the country have zoning laws. Those that do, do not cover all types of problems with neighbors. (See Chapter 2 for information on how to challenge a zoning law.)

MUNICIPAL ORDINANCES

Besides zoning laws, cities and counties often have other laws called *ordinances*, governing the use of property and peoples' behavior on the property. Some of these might be laws that forbid burning leaves, disturbing the peace, keeping dangerous animals, and so forth. The specific laws may be either *criminal laws* or *civil laws*. When there is a specific criminal law against behavior that is annoying, it will most likely be very easy to stop the behavior—just report the offending party to the proper authorities. If the law is civil it will probably say that you have the right to bring a private lawsuit in the matter. This will not be as easy, but pointing out to the offending party that he or she is violating the law may be of some help.

To find out if there are any laws about the problem that is annoying you, check both your city and county ordinances. These may also be available at your local library. If not, check your city, town, village, or county clerk's office. If you use the ones in your library, be sure they are complete and up-to-date. Municipal ordinances for many cities can also be found at:

www.findlaw.com/11stategov/municipal.html

STATE STATUTES

Besides municipal ordinances governing your rights, there may be state statutes that affect your rights. *Statutes* are usually composed of the hundreds or thousands of laws that were passed since the state was admitted to the union. In some states, they are not well-organized or indexed. Sometimes the title of a law does not accurately describe what is in the contents. Often the index is incomplete or inaccurate. This means you may have to comb the laws carefully if you want to be sure not to miss one that applies to your case.

For some cases, there may obscure laws that can give you relief. Taking your time to comb the statutes carefully may reward you with a solution. For instance, in Florida, there is an environmental law that overrules local restrictions on clotheslines. In California, there is a law that a seller of property must warn you about any noise problem. If not, you may be able to sue him!

Every state has a set of statutes. These may be just a couple volumes or over a hundred. They are usually available at your public library. If not, they will be in a law library that may be at your county courthouse. Most state statutes are also available on the Internet at:

www.law.cornell.edu/opinions.html#state

FEDERAL LAWS

There aren't many federal laws that control neighbor relations or property rights—but there are a few. The two most commonly affecting homeowners are:

1. *CERCLA—the short name for the Comprehensive Environmental Response, Compensation, and Liability Act.* This is a strong law used to combat pollution. It is often used to clean-up hazardous waste, such as gasoline leaking from service station storage tanks.

2. *The Noise Control Act* is contained in Title 42, United States Code, Sections 4901 through 4918. It provides for both criminal penalties and citizen suits, and covers railroads, motor carriers and others.

COMMON LAW PRINCIPLES

If there are no laws or restrictions forbidding an activity that is annoying you, then *common law principles* may offer some relief. The common law is law that has been created over the centuries by judges. This law is made up of the thousands of decisions made by judges in their court cases using *common law principles* of right and wrong on matters that were not covered by state statutes.

When things like fireworks, trains, and airplanes were first invented, there were no laws about how they should be used. When people started getting hurt and killed by them, the judges had to start making rules governing responsibility and liability for such injuries.

> **Example:** When someone was first brought into court for injuring someone by throwing fireworks into a crowd, his lawyer could argue that there was no law against throwing fireworks into crowds (since they were just invented). But the court could rule that throwing fireworks into a crowd was just like throwing a spear into a crowd, so the liability would be the same if anyone were hurt.

The common law is composed mostly of *civil law*, that is, law regarding relations between citizens. In most areas of this country, we do not have common law crimes because our courts have held that crimes must be very specifically spelled out in the statutes so that everyone may know ahead of time what is a crime.

Wrongful acts which are not crimes are called *torts*. When a person commits a tort against another person, he or she may be held *liable* in a civil court action for *damages* or may be ordered by the court to stop the activity.

It has been well-documented, that at this time, the civil court system is out-of-reach of a large percentage of Americans. The process is so slow and the lawyers' fees are so high that most people cannot afford a lengthy lawsuit. Therefore, a civil suit is probably not the best way to handle a neighbor dispute, unless it is small enough to be filed in *small claims court*.

Most American common law is based upon English common law. When each state (except Louisiana) joined the United States, it adopted the common law as it had existed in England. (Louisiana adopted French law.) This way the states did not have to create a completely new body of law. Everyone knew the principles of law under which they had conducted themselves in the past were still in effect. Then, as new cases came before the courts, new decisions were added to the common law.

Since each state has its own legal system, the common law in each state is not the same. In most areas, the law may be similar, but in some matters the states take divergent views. This is sometimes because of the nature of the population. For example, Montana may take a more individualistic approach than New York. In some matters, half of the states may follow one line of reasoning, while the other half follows another.

Over the years, as the population shifts, political parties change and judges are replaced. This often leads to a state changing its position. Occasionally, one state will take a totally new approach to a problem and other states will jump on the bandwagon, claiming it is the *progressive* approach or the *modern* view.

For this reason, and others, it would not be possible to tell you exactly what the law is at this moment in your state on a particular problem. What this book can do is give you the basic principles of law, some examples of how they have been applied in the past, and some guidance as to how to find specific cases and laws in your area.

NUISANCE LAW

When a person does something that is so annoying to his neighbors that it is illegal, it is called a *nuisance*. A nuisance is a *tort*; that is, a wrongful act or injury. Torts include such things as assault and battery, libel and slander, negligence and wrongful death.

There is no precise definition for the word nuisance. In fact the most famous author on the subject of torts has written, "There is perhaps no more impenetrable jungle in the entire law than that which surrounds the word 'nuisance.' It has meant all things to all men and has been applied indiscriminately to everything from an alarming advertisement to a cockroach baked in a pie." (So don't be surprised if this discussion seems a little confusing. It is also confusing to lawyers, judges, and law professors.)

Definition of Nuisance

To give you some idea as to what will be considered a legal nuisance, we can start with a few definitions.

- Blackstone, one of the earliest writers on English common law, described a nuisance as "Any thing that unlawfully worketh hurt, inconvenience, or damage." (American courts have expressed the opinion that it is hard to define exactly what falls into the category of nuisances.)
- The Wyoming Supreme Court said "There seems to be no definition of nuisance which is broad enough to include all those things that are nuisances, and so limited as to exclude those things to which the law gives another name."
- An Illinois court held that a nuisance includes everything that endangers life or health, gives offense to the senses, violates the laws of decency, or obstructs reasonable and comfortable use of property.
- The United States Supreme Court, at one point, described a nuisance as "a right thing in the wrong place—like a pig in the parlor instead of the barnyard."

Public nuisance. Nuisances can be classified as being either public or private, and this classification affects the legal rights of the parties concerned with the nuisance. A *public nuisance* is one that is a nuisance to the community at large. Some examples of public nuisances are:

- someone blocking a road;
- polluting a river used by the community;
- practicing medicine without a license; or,
- shooting-off fireworks in the streets.

Private nuisance. A nuisance that interferes with a specific person's use or enjoyment of his or her *own* property is called a *private nuisance.*

If a nuisance is judged to be a private nuisance, then the persons who are injured by it are entitled to take legal action to receive *compensation* for their *damages* and to stop the nuisance from continuing.

NOTE: *Because the notion of nuisance is based upon interests in land, persons who do not have an interest in the land, such as employees or guests do not have a right to take court action.*

Taking Action Against a Nuisance

If a nuisance is judged to be a public nuisance, then in most cases, only a governmental authority can take action to remedy it. (The logic behind this is that it would be too burdensome to people and businesses if every member of the public would be able to file a suit against them.)

One exception to this rule is that if some member of the public suffers some particular injury from the nuisance, then that person may seek compensation for his injury. In such cases, it is said that there is both a public nuisance and a private nuisance. However, determining when the private injury is enough to allow a person to sue has been a difficult question with which many courts have wrestled.

Another exception to this general rule is that in many states, specific laws have been passed that allow individual citizens to take legal action in the public interest to stop a public nuisance.

CONSTITUTIONAL RIGHTS

Constitutional rights can become an issue in neighbor relations in a few different ways. The most obvious is where a government agency is your neighbor. In such a case, most actions between you and the governmental entity would involve your constitutional rights.

Another way that a neighbor dispute could involve constitutional rights is when there is a state statute or local ordinance that controls some activity that becomes a problem between neighbors. In such a case, an important question would be whether the law complies with the state and federal constitutions. If not, it is unenforceable.

Some constitutional rights that might be invoked in a neighborhood dispute are: *freedom of speech, freedom of association, equal protection and equal treatment,* and *the right to just compensation for property taken by the government.* However, it is important to understand the meaning behind these rights. All of them have *some* limits.

Freedom of Speech

Constitutional rights are not absolute. The Supreme Court has ruled that when the government has a compelling interest and that interest cannot be achieved by a less restrictive means, a right guaranteed by the constitution may be limited. *Freedom of speech* is usually understood to mean that we as Americans can say anything at any time. But the limits to this freedom are numerous. We cannot yell "fire" in a crowded theater because that could cause a riot where people could be injured. We cannot say false things about people. That would be slander and we would have to pay for any damages caused by our false statements.

Speech that is advertising, has further limitations. Courts have ruled that *commercial speech* is subject to more limits than other types of speech. Thus, most laws that control advertising have been found to be constitutional.

Equal Protection and Equal Treatment

Equal protection requires that citizens in equal positions be treated equally. For example, courts will not enforce property restrictions that limit ownership based upon race. But, again, this right is not absolute. The courts have held that zoning laws are valid, even though they may give property owners who are next door to each other different rights in the use of their property. This is because the courts look at the objectives behind the laws and how the groups affected by the laws are classified. If the objectives and classifications are legitimate, then the laws are valid.

Just Compensation for Property Taken by the Government

The right to *just compensation for property taken by the government* was our country's answer to the habit of the king taking what he wanted—when he wanted it. Since kings had been thought to have divine rights, they were considered to have the ultimate ownership of everything and were allowed to take what they needed from people. Seeing how unfair this was, Americans evolved the principle that the government must pay a fair price whenever it took something from a citizen.

One of the first questions that then came up was how to define a "taking." When a government airport created so much noise that it ruined a neighbor's poultry business, this was held to be a "taking" of his property. Also, when a governmental body ruled that a person could no longer use his property for the purpose he intended, that too was a "taking" of the value of his property. Both of these types of takings required the government to pay the citizen compensation.

Due Process

There is also a right to *due process*. Actually, there are two types of due process, *substantive* and *procedural*.

Substantive due process. The power of the government to regulate the life of citizens is known as substantive due process. Like most areas of constitutional rights, *substantive due process* has changed and evolved over the two hundred years since the constitution was written. In the economic area, the Supreme Court has expanded the power of the government to control our lives. In the area of personal rights, the court has limited the power of the government. Undoubtedly, the changes will continue as the composition of the court changes.

Procedural due process. Steps the government must follow before it can deprive a person of "life, liberty, or property" is called *procedural due process*. The process depends upon what is being taken from the person. Where a person's life is being taken in a death penalty case, the person is entitled to the most carefully reviewed process. Where some value is taken from a person's land by the building of a jail next door, a less strict process is required.

Federal and State Government Actions

These constitutional rights apply to actions by both the federal government and state governments. They do not apply to actions by individuals.

> **Example:** A government action that lowers the value of your property can give you the constitutional right to just compensation, but a similar action by a private party would not. (It might give you the right to compensation under another legal theory such as *negligence*. As you will see in some of the cases, if you do not use the right theory when filing a lawsuit, you can lose, even if you are right and your neighbor is wrong.)

Constitutional rights can be asserted either in a suit *by* you against your neighbor or the government, or in a suit *against* you. In addition to the federal constitution, each state has it own constitution and many of these include additional rights not included in the federal constitution.

> **Example:** The constitution of the state of Washington contains a provision allowing a landowner to obtain damages if his land is damaged by excavations on the neighboring property. In some cases, these rights can be asserted against either the government or private parties.

–2–
PROBLEMS WITH PROPERTY AND ZONING

This chapter discusses some of the legal issues involved in the most common types of neighbor disputes dealing with property and zoning laws.

ADVERSE POSSESSION

There is an ancient principle of property law that if a person wrongfully holds onto another person's property long enough, then he or she can gain ownership of it. This is called *adverse possession*.

The *statute of limitations* forbids owners from suing to regain their land if they wait too long to do so. (A statute of limitation is a law setting a limit on how long a person can wait after an event before filing suit based on it.) This is based upon the rationale that after a certain period of time, it is too late to gather all the evidence and witnesses to prove a case in court. It also has the effect of making it easier to get *clear title* to a property.

For a person to legally gain title to a piece of property through adverse possession, he or she must:

◆ openly and notoriously take possession;
◆ hold exclusive possession of the property;
◆ hold possession continuously;
◆ hold possession without the owner's consent; and,
◆ hold the property for at least the period of time stated in the statute.

(Of course each of these points has been litigated numerous times and has been analyzed by several courts.)

Open and Notorious Possession

Possession of the property must be *open, notorious*, and *visible* to the owner of the property in order to cut off his rights. For instance, where a company took possession of a cave that extended under another person's land, the possession was not considered to be *open and notorious* to allow a claim of adverse possession.

Exclusive Possession

Exclusive possession means that possession is to the exclusion of the true owner of the property. The adverse possessor may be more than one person, such as husband and wife, and may share the possession such as by renting it to a tenant. In a case where the original owner of a strip of land mowed the land regularly, the person claiming adverse possession could not claim his possession was exclusive.

Where two people own a piece of property together, there can be no adverse possession unless one physically ousts the other. Merely taking over the duties and possession of the property is not enough.

Continuous Possession

The possession must be *continuous*. If a person claiming adverse possession abandons the property for a period of time, the period of possession starts over. However, if the property is only suitable for periodic use, such use *may* be considered continuous.

> In Mason County, Washington, a house was built on the wrong lot. Through some mistake it was built on the lot next to the one that it should have been built on. Over the years, the property was sold several times and each time the sellers transferred possession of the house, but deeded the lot next door. Eventually, the real owners of the property where the house was located, filed suit to have themselves declared the owners. The occupants of the house at that time claimed that since they and their predecessors had occupied the house for years, they had acquired title to the property by adverse possession. The

actual owners pointed out that the land was a summer house and that it was therefore not occupied continuously as is required for adverse possession. They won the case.

However, the occupants appealed and the ruling was reversed. The appeals court ruled that when a property is a summer house, continuous occupancy could consist of occupancy every summer, not all year round.

Without Consent of the Owner

It is said that an adverse possessor must hold possession to the property *hostile* to the owner. This means that the person must be in possession *without consent of the owner*. In some areas, the courts require that the adverse possessor must have some basis for his claim to the land, but most states allow any *squatter* to make a claim.

A majority of the states use an *objective test*—looking at the actions of the possessor to determine if the possession is adverse. But other states use a *subjective test*—looking into the mind of the possessor to see if he has a good faith belief that he has title to the property.

When a man died, he had no will and so his land passed to his widow and his children. Shortly, thereafter, one of his children died without a will and her interest passed to her husband and children. Her mother, her siblings, and her husband all deeded the property to her brother. Thirty-four years later, the parties realized that the deed was not effective to convey her children's interest. The brother filed suit to clear his title, but the court said that he could not claim adverse possession because nothing was done that would serve as notice to the children that he was claiming adversely.

Statutory Period

Adverse possession is governed by state statutes. The time period in the various states may vary from seven to twenty years or more. Some states have additional laws that impose other requirements on adverse possession. Such things as the adverse possessor must have paid the taxes on the property during the period; that he or she must have some sort of deed to the property before making the claim; or, that he or she have a good faith belief in the ownership of the property.

EASEMENTS

In some situations, property owners need or desire to make use of property owned by a neighbor. The need will usually be for physical access to the property, but it can also be for water rights, electrical lines, a better view, or some other benefit. When neighbors disagree on the extent of these rights, they often end up in court where their rights are determined by common law principles of easement developed over several hundred years.

An *easement* is the right of one party to use land owned by another party. For instance, a person whose property is not on a road may have an easement across another property to use as access to the road.

Categories of Easements

Easements can be *appurtenant* or *in gross*. *Appurtenant* means that the easement is a benefit to another particular piece of land. An easement for access would be an example of appurtenant. When an easement is appurtenant, the property that owns the easement right is said to be the *dominant estate*. The one subject to the easement is said to be the *servient estate*. An easement *in gross* is one that can benefit anyone without relation to a piece of property, such as an easement giving someone the right to use a lake for fishing and recreation.

An easement can also be either *affirmative* or *negative*. An affirmative easement means that the holder of the easement can do something on the other person's land, such as cross over it. A negative easement means that the servient estate is not allowed to do some act, such as build higher than a certain height.

Under English common law there were only a limited number of types of easements, such as for access to property, for water, for light, or for air. But American courts have recognized easements for all kinds of things. Some examples are easements for scenic view, for grazing cattle, or for the right to flood land.

Creation of Easements

There are four traditional ways that easements can be created:

1. by express grant;
2. by necessity;
3. by implication; and,
4. by prescription.

In addition, easements may be created by laws passed by the states.

An *easement by express grant* can be created by a *deed* or by a *will*. One property owner may pay another for a deed of an easement over his land. Or, someone deeding property to another person may state in the deed that he reserves an easement to himself and his heirs. A person leaving property by will may create easements as part of the *disposition of his property*.

An *easement by necessity* is recognized if a person has no other access to his property. For instance, a piece of land located on a road is divided into front and back halves. If the back half has no other access to a road, then a court would rule that the parcel in back has an *easement by necessity* across the front parcel for access to the road.

An *easement by implication* is one that is implied from the circumstances, even though it has not been put in writing. This would be similar to an easement by necessity, except that there is a requirement that the easement area have been used continuously prior to the severance of the properties.

An *easement by prescription* is one that is created by constant use of property over a long period of time. (This is similar to adverse possession, discussed earlier in this chapter.) The basic rule is that if a person, *open and notoriously* uses another's property without permission for a long enough period of time, that person can acquire some legal rights to the property.

In extraordinary cases, state legislatures have created easements to protect traditional rights.

> 🏠 *A statute was passed to protect the ancient gathering rights of the native Hawaiians when the idea of property ownership was introduced there. Under the law, certain Hawaiians can enter the private property of others to gather specific leaves and herbs. However, these rights are very limited. When a person who no longer lived in the area attempted to assert his rights—his claim was denied. The court ruled that the rights only belonged to those who lived adjacent to the land.*

Scope of Rights

Disputes often arise when one party wishes to expand or limit the use of an easement. This can happen when the holder of the easement wants to start making a much greater use of the easement or when the owner of the *servient property* wants to use his property in a way that will limit the rights of the easement owner.

The court decisions on easements, over the years, have usually recognized the principle that easements are limited to their original uses. However, they may be expanded by reasonable development and modernization.

> 🏠 *An easement was acquired by prescription across the property of a railroad in Illinois for access to a house and stable. Later, two additional buildings were built on the property—each with two dwelling units. Suit was brought against the railroad to restore the path the people used across the easement. The court noted that although most cases hold that the rights in an easement gained by pre-*

scription cannot be enlarged, in this case the change was not in kind of use, but in quantity of people. It held that the people had a right to continued use of the easement.

🏠 *A couple bought a lot next to their property so that they could build a new residence straddling the two lots. Neighbors claimed that using the easement to access the additional parcel was beyond the scope of the easement. The couple sued and won the right to use the easement. The neighbors appealed and the judgment was reversed.*

In this case, the couple appealed to the Washington Supreme Court and the original opinion was reinstated. The couple was given the right to use the easement even though they then owned an additional lot because there was no additional burden placed on the neighbor's property. The easement would still be used only for access to a single family home.

🏠 *Shady Shore was a subdivision on Lake Huron, described as the most beautiful of all Port Huron's beautiful beaches. The lots were large and intended for expensive single-family dwellings. There was no public roadway through the plat for access to the beach, as it was the intention that the beach would be exclusively for the use of the lot owners. Each lot owner held an easement for access to the beach. Developers bought three lots and subdivided them into twenty-six lots. They put up a sign welcoming people to the beach and sold several of the lots. The cottages built on the lots were rented out for short periods of time. The people visiting the beach would make commotion on the beach that would annoy the long-term residents of the neighborhood.*

In this case, the Supreme Court of Michigan found that this increased the burden on the easement beyond that contemplated at the time the easement was created. It was meant for three families to have access to the beach, not twenty-six. The court approved a permanent injunction against use of the easement.

The owner of the land subject to the easement can still use the land for any purpose that does not affect the rights of the owner of the easement.

> **Example:** The electric company may have an easement across part of your lot for transmission lines. But, you can still use the land in any way that does not interfere with their easement.

Transfer of Easements

The general rule is that easements appurtenant are automatically transferred with the dominant property. An easement appurtenant cannot be severed from the land and transferred to a third party without the consent of the land the easement crosses.

Easements in gross usually cannot be transferred. They may end up in the hands of numerous parties and heirs of parties that would make it difficult to maintain clear title to the land. An exception to this is that easements of a commercial nature may be transferred. Also, in a few jurisdictions, all easements may be freely transferred.

Termination of Easements

In most cases, an easement is permanent and will last forever. However, there are certain circumstances when an easement can be terminated. Some of these are:

   ◆ mutual agreement;
   ◆ abandonment;
   ◆ merger;
   ◆ prescription; and,
   ◆ forfeiture.

🏠 *A parcel of land in Atherton, California had access by way of an easement over the land of some neighbors. The owners of the parcel also owned a larger parcel next door, but that parcel had access through another road. When the owners of the parcel subdivided the two parcels into twenty-nine lots, they made the sole access to the property across the easement. In a legal action by the neighbors, the court ruled that the owners of the parcel could not expand the use of the easement by adding all of the lots of the second parcel. By dedicating the subdivision roads to the public, they lost their right to use the easement.*

UTILITIES

Generally, no one, including utility companies, can come onto your property or run pipes or wires across your property without your permission. The United States Supreme Court issued an important decision on this issue. New York had passed a law that allowed cable TV companies to put their wires on private property upon paying the sum of $1 to the owner. A woman who owned a building sued the company that put its cables on her building saying it was a violation of her rights to just compensation under the Fifth Amendment to the United States Constitution.

The City of New York joined the case saying it was important that they have a right to control cable TV and the trial court ruled for the cable company. The woman appealed to the highest court in New York and it also ruled for the cable company. But then she went to the United States Supreme Court and won. The court ruled that forcing landowners to allow cables to be run on their property was addressed under the Fifth Amendment. Therefore, they must receive just compensation for it.

Easements

In most situations, electrical wires, sewer and water lines, telephone and TV cable are run along *easements*. Easements are rights granted by property owners allowing others to use part or all of the property.

Sometimes easements are granted by each landowner, separately. Sometimes they are put on all lots in a subdivision when the streets are first laid out.

> **Example:** A plat of a subdivision may have an easement across the rear five feet of each lot. This may be noted by lines on the plat or merely mentioned in small print in a paragraph at the bottom. It can also be mentioned in any restrictions filed for the subdivision, or on the first deed give to each owner who bought a lot.

When an owner sells his property, he or she usually gives a warranty deed guaranteeing that the owner giving the purchaser has *good title*. If there are any easements on the property, the deed should make the warranty, but make exception to those easements. If it does not, the seller may be liable for *breach of warranty*. To avoid liability, sellers' attorneys often add a clause to the deed that the property is subject to "easements and restrictions of record." As a buyer, always inquire into what exactly they are. (An easement down the middle of you lot can make it worthless.)

If someone is attempting to use part of your property for utility cables or pipes, ask them for proof of exactly where they think their easement is located. You should compare this to the easements disclosed by your title insurance policy or title search. If it is unclear where the easement is located, you might need to hire a surveyor to prepare a drawing of your property.

If the utility company is using part of your property outside of the easement, you can stop them or make them pay for it. If your title insurance policy does not disclose the easement (or states the easement in a general way, "subject to easements of record"), then you may be able to get them to pay you for the value of the easement.

BUILDINGS AND STRUCTURES

There are several ways in which a building or other structure can cause problems for neighbors. It may be dangerous, unsightly, or lower the value of the neighborhood.

A building or structure that is merely unsightly is much more difficult to remedy. While many areas have attempted to regulate the appearance of property, it has been harder to justify these laws in the courts. While safety is generally accepted to be a legitimate governmental concern, beauty (which, of course, is in the eye of the beholder) has not been.

If the problem causing a property to be unsightly is also dangerous, such as junk attracting rats or peeling paint that might contain lead, it may be possible to get a health or building inspector to take action. Otherwise, it will not be easy to take legal action. Unless a building violates a zoning rule or other restriction on the property, there is no limit of how high it can be built.

In platted subdivisions, the property restrictions often offer stringent controls on what types of structures can be built. As explained in the beginning of this book, such restrictions are voluntarily placed on the property by the original owners and each purchaser must comply with them. Purchasers are deemed to be aware of them, even if they have never actually seen them.

Often, subdivision restrictive covenants will provide that anyone violating the rules will have to pay all costs and attorneys' fees in any lawsuit that must be brought to enforce the restrictions.

> 🏠 *A man bought three lots and a partially completed house on Hilton Head Island, South Carolina. He had a set of construction plans approved by the Architectural Board of Sea Pines Plantation. He then proceeded to erect an additional flagpole, a jacuzzi, and a satellite antenna on the roof along with other unapproved structures such as a beach walkway, shower, fence, gate, and additional trees. The trial court ordered him to remove the items as he was in violation of the restrictive covenant.*

In this case, the Supreme Court of South Carolina held that the restrictive covenants were enforceable; the covenants were not arbitrarily or discriminatorily enforced; the flagpole, jacuzzi, and satellite dish were prohibited by the covenant; and that the homeowner had breached the covenants by failing to obtain approval for landscape modifications and by obstructing the view of other lot owners.

Encroachment

An *encroachment* exists where a structure on one person's property crosses the property line onto the neighboring owner's property. An encroachment may be as small as a roof hanging one inch over the line or as big as an entire house being built on the wrong lot.

Example: The Wells Amusement Co. in Anniston, Alabama added an amusement center to its property. It used the wall of a neighboring building to attach its roof. Apparently, the company wanted to avoid the cost of building its own wall and was using the side of the building as the interior wall of its amusement center. The court held that this was an encroachment and it was ordered removed.

🏠 *When a woman built a poured concrete wall on her property in Hammond, Indiana, no paper was used to separate her wall from the adjacent building. The concrete ran into all of the cracks and crevices in her neighbor's wall. In 99% of the cases, this would have gone unnoticed forever. However, the street in front of the properties was widened. The neighbor needed to have his two-story brick building moved back. After all preparations were made, including a new foundation, it was discovered that the two buildings were stuck together. The neighbor sued to force the woman to remove the concrete. The court ruled that concrete filling the cracks in a wall would constitute a trespass. However, since the court believed that neighbor knew about the wall and allowed the concrete to be poured in that manner, it did not order the trespass to be removed.*

If an encroachment is left unchallenged for a long enough period of time, the owner of it may acquire a permanent right to maintain it. This is called a *right by prescription*. It is similar to adverse possession and often the time period required is twenty years.

In some areas there are laws regulating the rights of the parties in the case of encroachments. For instance, in New York, there is a law that states that if an encroachment is of six inches or less, no court action can be brought more than one year after the encroachment starts.

An encroachment has been considered as both a nuisance and a trespass, but it more technically falls into the definition of a trespass. As a trespass, it entitles the owner to monetary damages, whether he or she has suffered any actual losses or not. This also means that the *doctrine of de minimis* (the law is not concerned with trifles) does not apply. An encroachment of one inch is considered serious.

🏠 *In order to protect his property in Pulaski County, Arkansas from water running off his neighbor's property, a landowner had a 140-foot-long stone and cement wall built. Unfortunately, twenty-six feet of it encroached a few inches onto his neighbor's property. The neighbor filed suit to require removal of the wall. The trial judge ruled that there was an encroachment, but that it was minimal and that the landowner should not have to go through the trouble and expense of removing it.*

In this case, the Supreme Court of Arkansas disagreed, saying that the doctrine that the law does not concern itself with trifles does not apply to invasion of real estate. It ordered the wall moved.

Removing the encroachment. An owner whose property is encroached upon has the right to personally remove the encroachment, as long as he or she does not cause any additional damages.

> The Bijou Theater in Racine, Wisconsin had a gutter that projected over the property next door. When the neighbor made plans to build a taller building, he asked several times that the gutter be removed. Finally, his workmen had to remove it. In doing so, an opening was left in the roof that allowed rain and snow to get in. The neighbor was not held liable for the damage because the work had been done properly and he had a right to remove the gutter.

If the owner does not wish to or cannot remove the encroachment, he or she can bring a court action. This would be a civil action. In the court action, the owner could force the encroachment to be removed or he or she could seek monetary damages.

> A man in Massachusetts built a concrete block garage on his property with a concrete roof and a large driveway. It was built in such a way that water from the roof and driveway poured onto his neighbor's property. She hired a surveyor who discovered that the garage was built about two inches over the property line. She sued asking that he be forced to remove the garage from her property; stop draining water into her yard; and, to not park more than two cars in his garage.

In this case, the court ordered that the garage owner stop the water from draining on her property. Since moving the garage would cost 100 times the value of the two inches of property, it held that he would not have to move it if he paid her the value of the property. She appealed. The Supreme Court of Massachusetts held that the garage was trespassing and must be moved. But it said that parking three cars in the garage was not a nuisance.

🏠 *A man owned a lot in Washington, D.C. The adjoining lot was home to the Atlantic Building. Part of the rear wall of the Atlantic Building was built upon the lot owner's land. When he began to erect a building on his lot, he sought to use the Atlantic Building's wall as a party wall. The owner agreed, but later notified him that the wall was not a party wall. When he dug trenches in order to build his own wall, he discovered that the footing of the wall encroached upon his land about two feet along the length of the wall. He began using the wall as a party wall and sued to force the building owner to remove the encroachment. The court held it would not force the defendant to remove the footing since he elected to use the wall as a party wall. It held he could remove the footings, without impairing the wall, at his own cost.*

🏠 *A concrete bulkhead built by a woman on her property in Seattle, Washington, settled a few inches onto the property of her neighbor. He filed suit and was awarded $1 in damages. She was ordered to move the bulkhead within sixty days. On appeal, she argued that the bulkhead was doing no damage, but would be very costly to remove, so the doctrine of de minimis non curat lex (the law does not concern itself with trifles) should apply.*

In this case, the court held that on a city lot, an irregular lot could result in serious building complications. The doctrine could not apply in this case.

🏠 *After buying a lot in Sacramento County, California, a man discovered that his neighbor's carport and hedge encroached on a 4.5 foot triangle of his property. He brought a suit for removal of the encroachment. The court refused to order removal, but ordered the neighbor to pay* *him $250 to purchase the property from him. Not wanting to sell the property, he appealed. The appeals court noted that where there is great hardship in removing an encroachment, it will not be ordered. However, in this case, there was no extreme hardship. It noted that while his driveway would not be wide enough for a car, he could still use the alley for access to his lot.*

🏠 *When the Odd Fellows Lodge in Lane County, Oregon and the owner of the surrounding property at Fisherman's Wharf discovered that their buildings overlapped on each others' properties, they exchanged five-foot strips of land. However, the surveyor did not notice that the lodge was built at an angle and that it encroached a few inches at one end. A subsequent owner of the surrounding property noticed that the eaves of the building encroached even more and that the building leaned against his building. He filed suit. The court ordered the lodge to jack-up its building to stop the leaning and to remove the eaves. The court declined to order the entire building be moved to eliminate the encroachment on the rear of the building, as the cost would be great and the benefit would be small.*

Usually the person who is liable for an encroachment is the owner of the property. But in some cases, if a contractor or tenant cause the encroachment and the owner was blameless, then the proper party to sue would be the person who caused it.

🏠 *A man owned a building in Madison, Wisconsin when the neighbor contracted to build a theater on the lot it owned next door. The contractor subcontracted the excavation and masonry work. After excavation, part of the soil caved in. When the concrete was poured, it extended on to the building owner's property. In a suit against the owner, contractor, and subcontractor, the court held that while the contractor would not have any liability to the adjacent owner, the subcontractor could be liable if his negligence caused the encroachment.*

Contractors

One of the greatest risks to the homeowner, (and one least known), is the risk that the home can be sold for failure to pay for materials or repairs on the property. In order to protect contractors, workers, and material suppliers, most states have laws that allow these parties to file a *lien* against a property if they are not paid for goods or services. If the lien is then not paid, a suit can be filed in court and the property can be sold to pay the lien.

I had an elderly neighbor who enjoyed remodeling her house every few years. She also had the unfortunate combination of being a perfectionist and wanting to get everything for the lowest possible price. Inevitably, she got into disputes with contractors whose low-priced, imperfect work did not meet her standards. After her last remodeling job, she refused to pay the contractor. He filed a lien and a court action to foreclose on her home. The court ordered that her $80,000 home be sold to pay the $3,000 lien. She was told that she could lose her house if she didn't pay, but at this point she was suffering from dementia. Fortunately, a court-appointed guardian paid the lien and lady's house was saved.

Before you have any work done on your property, become familiar with the laws covering workers and material men's liens. *Some* of the laws are not very supportive of the owners. Under some laws, the owner can pay the contractor in full for the work. However, if the contractor fails to pay the workers or pay for the materials, the owner of the property may have to pay them, too. The only way to avoid paying double under those kinds of laws is to get the *subcontractors* (workers and material suppliers) to sign *releases*. Also, under some laws, you must file a notice in the courthouse before work begins. You then receive notice of all the parties supplying goods or services to your property.

Laws covering liens are different in each state and they are amended frequently. To protect yourself, check with your building department on what the procedures are in your specific area. Some of them have pamphlets or booklets explaining exactly what homeowners must do to protect against liens.

NOTE: *Be sure to read any papers that come from the court regarding a worker' lien. If you do not respond properly, your house can be sold without your knowing it. Check with a lawyer if you do not understand the court papers or if you are not sure of your homeowner rights.*

Chimney

Chimneys present special problems because unless they are taller than surrounding structures, they will not work properly. The way they work is that air passing across the top of the chimney creates a vacuum pulling the smoke out. If a neighboring building is taller and blocks the wind, the smoke may not properly ventilate or it may blow into the taller building.

Because of this situation, some areas have laws that require owners of new buildings that are taller than neighboring chimneys to pay the cost of making the chimneys taller than their building. New York City is an area that has this kind of law. (Of course neighbors have gotten into lawsuits over the exact requirements of the law.)

A company built a building in the Bronx. The owner built a metal smoke stack on the shorter building next door. Over the years, the smoke stack rusted and did not work as well and caused damage to the shorter building. The owner sued for replacement of the smoke stack and for repair of the damages. The court ruled that while the owner of the taller building was liable for repairing the smoke stack, it was not liable for other damages that the neighbor had allowed to happen by not taking action sooner.

RESIDENTS

There are no laws in this country controlling the types of people who live in different neighborhoods. Such laws would violate the *equal protection clause* of the United States Constitution and many state constitutions as well. However, some private restrictive covenants that regulate the types of people in a neighborhood have been upheld. Some zoning laws have had the effect of controlling types of people who move into an area.

🏠 *Many years ago, it was not unusual for restrictions to be placed on subdivisions that stated the properties could be transferred only to persons of the Caucasian race or not to persons of the Negro or Mongoloid races. In 1948, the United States Supreme Court held that the courts in this country could not enforce these covenants. To get around this, the courts started awarding monetary damages against anyone violating such covenants. Then in 1953, the Supreme Court ruled that courts could not grant monetary damages for these types of violations either. It reasoned that the government of the United States can not aid an individual in an act that would be unconstitutional for the government to do.*

NOTE: *At that time, there was no law against property owners voluntarily enforcing such a prohibition. However, the subsequently adopted civil rights and fair housing acts have made such restrictions illegal.*

Illegal Restraint on Alienation

One type of control that has been upheld by the courts has been the right of some homeowner groups to control the sale of other units. This has often been held to be legal for condominiums and for cooperative apartments. However, when applied to homes, it has been rejected as an illegal limit on the salability of property (a *restraint on alienation*).

> 🏠 *In 1940, a couple purchased land in Wayne and Monroe Counties, Pennsylvania, including Lake Watawga. When they divided and sold the land as lots, they put a restriction on the property that all purchasers must be members of the Lake Watawga Association and that other members of the association would vote to determine whether a prospective purchaser could become a member. In 1958, after the husband passed away, his widow filed a suit to declare the restrictions void so that she could sell some of the land to persons who were not members of the association. The association then filed a suit against her to stop the selling of her property to anyone not belonging to the association. They won and she appealed to the Pennsylvania Supreme Court.*

In this case, it held that the restrictions were void because they restricted the ability of people to freely sell their land. The court also held that members of the association could, by whim, deny any person the right to buy property.

Right of First Refusal
To avoid the problem of causing illegal restraint on alienation, some associations have instead created a *right of first refusal* to a homeowners' group to purchase a property that is to be sold to someone they find objectionable. This has often been held to be legal.

> 🏠 *York Center is a subdivision in Du Page County, Illinois. It has seventy-two families, all of whom are members of the York Center Community Cooperative, Inc., their neighborhood association. Under the rules of their association, no member could sell their interest until the cooperative had an opportunity to bid. Any interest sold on the open market, could be*

bought back by the association. When one couple refused to convey their interests to the association, it sued. The Illinois Supreme Court held that while restrictions controlling the right to sell property are usually void, where they are reasonable and useful in attaining accepted social ends, as in this case, they would be legal.

Single-Family Residences

Another type of controls that affects the people in a neighborhood is restricting the property to single-family residences. This can be done by deed restrictions or by zoning laws. Such restrictions and laws are usually upheld, but some courts have weakened them by broadening the definition of *family*.

🏠 *An ordinance of the Village of Belle Terre, New York limited land use to single-family dwellings. It defined family as people related by blood, marriage, or adoption or no more than two unrelated persons living and cooking together. When a homeowner rented a house to six unrelated students, the village prosecuted them and won. The homeowner appealed and the law was found to be unconstitutional. The village then appealed to the United States Supreme Court. The court held that the law was reasonable and that it bore a rational relationship to a permissible state objective.*

🏠 *A woman lived in East Cleveland with her son and two grandsons who were first cousins. In 1973, she was convicted of violating a city ordinance that limited occupancy to a single family. Under the rationale of the earlier case, her conviction was upheld.*

In this case, on appeal to the United States Supreme Court, the law was held to be unconstitutional. The difference, the court held, was that in this case, the law dictated living arrangements within families and made it a crime for a grandmother to live with a grandchild. It noted the sanctity of the family in America and said that the history and tradition of the country compel a larger conception of the family.

> 🏠 *In 1980, the New York City/Long Island County Services Group leased a home in the hamlet of Crane Neck for use as a home for eight severely retarded adults. In addition to the residents, there were sixteen staff persons working at the property. This upset other residents in the area, since the property had restrictions on its use limiting it to single-family residences. The neighbors filed suit and the trial court found that such use of the property was not a use as a single-family residence.*

In this case, the appeals court reversed, finding that in New York, eight severely retarded adults and sixteen staff members could constitute a family. The case then went to the New York Supreme Court. It said that such a group was not a single family, but that it didn't matter. It held that when the state wants to do something important like providing a home for retarded persons, it can ignore private deed restrictions.

Zoning Regulations

Some areas have attempted to use zoning to exclude certain people from the area. This is done by requiring that lots or homes to be of a certain (large) size. It has also occurred when banning multifamily or publicly subsidized housing. Generally, federal courts have not forbidden such exclusionary zoning, but several state courts have held them to be illegal under state constitutions.

One consideration that is looked at is whether the zoning has an *exclusionary purpose* or merely an *exclusionary effect*. If the purpose of a zoning rule is to discriminate racially, then it will be held invalid. If it is found that there is a legitimate purpose to the rule, but that it inadvertently has a discriminatory effect, then it is usually held to be valid.

> 🏠 *In the early 1970s, the local chapter of the NAACP and others brought a suit against the Township of Mt. Laurel, New Jersey, complaining that its zoning plan excluded low-income individuals from the township. The township was comprised of expensive homes. The Supreme Court of New Jersey ruled that under the state constitution, the township had a duty to provide for a fair share of the region's low-income population.*

In this case, eight years later, the township was again brought before the New Jersey Supreme Court with a complaint that nothing had been done by the township to allow low-income individuals to move into the area. In an opinion of over one hundred pages, complete with several pages of maps, the court laid out a detailed plan. The plan included changes in zoning, incentives for builders of low-income housing, and special judges to administer the program, in order to force the towns in the area to accept low-income housing.

> 🏠 *A nonprofit housing developer contracted to buy land in Arlington Heights, Illinois to build low-income housing, contingent upon rezoning of the property. The rezoning was denied and the company sued, claiming the reason for the denial was racial discrimination. The United States Supreme Court held that the fact that the zoning had a racial impact was not the sole matter to consider. For the zoning to be held invalid, there must have been proof of a racially discriminatory intent or purpose. In this case, there was a legitimate purpose other than racial discrimination.*

🏠 *The Cleburne Living Center brought suit against the city of Cleburne, Texas, because the zoning law did not permit it to start a group home for the mentally retarded. The suit ended up in the Supreme Court of the United States. The justices of the court filed three different opinions. A majority of the justices ruled that mental retardation was not a suspect classification that required a strict scrutiny, but that the law violated equal protection anyway, since there was no rational basis for excluding the group home from the area.*

Sights. Until recent years, government attempts to control the *look* of a neighborhood have generally not been seen favorably by the courts. When the United States Supreme Court first approved zoning laws in 1926, it held that if the objectives of zoning were the health, safety, morals, and welfare of the citizens, it was valid.

The first crack in the rules was when cases began to accept aesthetics as one of several objectives that could form the basis for a zoning scheme. As governmental regulation has become more acceptable in more and more areas of our lives, the courts have held that aesthetics could be the sole basis for a zoning regulation.

🏠 *The city of Baltimore, Maryland was so successful in limiting the size of signs in the Charles Center area that it decided to try to achieve uniformity in the whole downtown district. In 1970, just before the expiration of a five-year moratorium in the sign ordinance, ten firms filed suit attacking the validity of the ordinance regulating signs.*

In this case, the trial judge ruled that the ordinance was invalid and the city appealed. The Court of Appeals of Maryland agreed that since the sole purpose of the ordinance was aesthetics, it was not a permissible use of the police powers.

🏠 *The county of Monterey, California, passed a zoning ordinance that required removal of billboards within one year. A company that owned several billboards in the county, brought suit against the county to keep it from enforcing the law. The trial court agreed and found the law to be unenforceable.*

In this case, the county appealed and the Supreme Court of California held that the law could be enforced as to thirty-one billboards that the company had fully amortized under the IRS regulations, but that it could not be enforced as to eleven signs that had not been amortized. The Court said that there was nothing wrong with the fact that the company would have to pay about $139 per billboard to remove them.

🏠 *The city of San Diego enacted an ordinance banning many types of billboards and signs in the city. The objective was eliminating hazards to pedestrians and motorists and to improve the appearance of the city. The ordinance prohibited most types of signs except on-site commercial signs. Several companies engaged in outdoor advertising sued and the trial court ruled the law unconstitutional. The appeals court agreed, but the Supreme Court of California reversed, holding the law to be valid.*

In this case, the companies appealed to the United States Supreme Court that reversed the California Supreme Court. It held that while the control of commercial signs was valid, the ban on noncommercial signs was invalid under the First and Fourteenth Amendments to the U.S. Constitution.

In some cases, special laws have been passed to combat sights that were especially disturbing to the city fathers.

🏠 *To protest the high taxes of the city of Rye, New York, a couple erected a clothesline, filled with old clothes, in front of their house on the corner of Rye Beach and Forest Avenues. During each succeeding year, they would add another clothesline, including underwear, old uniforms, tattered clothing, rags, and scarecrows. By 1961, there were six clotheslines—three on Forest and three on Rye Beach.*

In August, 1961, the city passed an ordinance prohibiting clotheslines in a front or side yard abutting a street and prosecuted the couple for maintaining their clotheslines. The city won in the trial court and the couple appealed, claiming that the law infringed upon their constitutional rights. Both the county court and New York Supreme Court sided with the city.

If an unsightly property is not against a zoning law or building code, there is probably not much that can be done in civil court. In order to constitute a nuisance, it would have to cause substantial injury to a nearby owner.

🏠 *The city of Indianola, Iowa, established a dump in an agricultural area within the city limits. Over the years, it was enlarged by adding more land. Later, a man purchased a large tract of land next to the dump and began developing it into a subdivision. The man's own home was in the subdivision and just 120 yards from the dump. The dump was an open type. The dump was in plain view from the subdivision. Rats and flies were attracted to the dump and smoke was given off night and day from the burning of garbage and animal bodies. He filed suit and won an injunction ordering that the dump stop operations.*

In this case, the city appealed and the Supreme Court of Iowa ruled that as long as the dump put up a fence; stopped burning animal bodies; and, took action to reduce the rats and flies, the dump would be allowed to continue operations. The court found it important that the dump had been in operation for many years before the houses were built. It also found that the dump provided an essential service to the community.

DANGEROUS SITUATIONS EXISTING ON PROPERTY

Where a dangerous situation exists on a piece of property, the simplest solution is to seek help through health, zoning, or building officials. Codes in many areas are becoming so strict that anything remotely dangerous will probably be a violation.

If the situation does not violate any regulatory code, then the question of whether there is a civil remedy will depend upon several factors. One is whether the danger is to persons on the premises or off the premises. Another factor is whether the dangerous condition naturally occurred on the land or was artificially created. A third factor is whether the situation is normally dangerous or unnecessarily dangerous.

> There were large rocks located on a bluff that were liable to break away and fall. A group of neighbors filed suit claiming the rocks were a nuisance to the public. On one occasion, a five-ton piece of rock broke away and fell down the slope crashing into a neighbor's home, causing damage. The cause of the fall was weather, not any mining or quarrying operations. The court held that the owner was not liable for damages caused by the rocks since the falling was due to natural causes.

When the dangerous condition is artificially created, the courts will look to whether the condition is abnormally dangerous. Some activities, such as high voltage lines, foundries, and mining operations are normally dangerous activities. They will usually not be stopped by a neighbor's complaint because they are considered valuable to society. If an activity is abnormally dangerous, it may become either a public or a private nuisance. It may be stopped by governmental action or by a private law suit.

🏠 *The Grand River Dam Authority entered into a contract with the city of Wagoner, Oklahoma to supply electricity to the city and to construct transmission lines. Knowing how eager some people are to file lawsuits, Grand River first filed its own petition with the Supreme Court of Oklahoma. It requested a ruling on the legality of its contract. The court ruled that its contract was legal and that the property owners adjacent to streets where the transmission lines would be built could not claim that the power lines were a nuisance.*

🏠 *After harvesting his crop of grass seed on fifty-five acres near I-5 in Linn County, Oregon, a farmer burned the field. Subsequently, the fire spread to other properties, including that of two neighbors, whose damages amounted to $8,017.00. The Industrial Forestry Association, the Oregon Seed Council, the Oregon Seed Trade Association, the Oregon Rygrass Growers Association, the Oregon Farm Bureau Federation, and the Field Burning Defense Committee sent lawyers into the action. The trial court held that if the person burning the field was careful and the fire was caused by something such as an unexpected whirlwind rather than negligence, then there would be no liability.*

In this case, the Oregon Supreme Court said that burning a field was an abnormally dangerous activity and where one of two innocent persons must suffer, it should be the one who engaged in the dangerous activity.

🏠 *In 1916, four days before Christmas, a fire started at an oil. association in Abilene, Texas when an employee lit an oil stove and left it unattended for half an hour. The fire ignited 12,000 gallons of kerosene and 300 gallons of gasoline on the premises. The mixture then ran out of the building and into the street. As it flowed down the street, its path was blocked by an earthen dam thrown up by employees of the oil company. After reaching the dam, it flowed toward some residences and set them ablaze. Gilbert McGuffey lost his houses and their contents in the fire. He sued the oil association, but lost because the court held that the earthen dam was the cause of his fire.*

In this case, on appeal the court held that the storage of dangerous materials could constitute a nuisance and that he was entitled to a new trial on that basis.

A man was visiting a neighbor in Hudson County, New Jersey. He was tinkering with an automobile in the yard, when a four by eight foot icy mass over eight inches thick slid off the roof of the neighbor's garage and seriously injured him. The court held the neighbor liable because the structure of the roof was not a natural one and the sliding of the ice was foreseeable.

Situations Involving Children

Situations where there was a condition that was dangerous only to persons who enter a piece of property, usually come up only after someone is injured. For adults, this situation can be avoided by never entering the dangerous property. However, if a dangerous situation exists on a neighbor's property, it may attract children who are not wise enough to avoid it. Unfortunately, if the situation does not violate a specific law, there is probably not a civil remedy for it.

The best advice that can be given to neighbors concerned about a dangerous situation is to warn the owner (and the tenant if the property is leased) of the hazard and to point out that children may be attracted to it. This should be done in a letter sent by certified mail. The letter is important because once a person is on notice of a danger, there is a greater chance of holding him liable.

Dangerous Buildings

A building or structure that is dangerous is the easiest problem to solve. Whether it is in danger of falling down or causing risk to children who play in the area, the remedy is to call building, health, or zoning officials. In most cases, it is a violation of some code for the structure to remain in a dangerous condition.

Even if the structure does not violate some specific code, it still may be considered by a court to be a nuisance. If it is a danger to the public at large, it may be a public nuisance. If it is a danger just to the neighbors, it may be a private nuisance.

> *While a woman was in Europe, a building she owned in Detroit, Michigan, was found by the city inspectors to be in imminent danger of collapse. The city took action to begin the demolition, but before it could do so, the building collapsed and damaged the property next door. The neighbor sued the owner for having a dangerous condition constituting a nuisance. However, the court ruled that the actions by the city in taking control of the building relieved her of her liability.*

Excavations and Support

It is an established principle of American property law that a landowner has a duty to maintain lateral support to adjoining properties. This means that you cannot dig a hole on your land if it will cause your neighbor's land to cave in. If you do need to dig a hole, such as an excavation for a basement, it is your duty to shore up your neighbor's property and keep it from caving in.

A limit to the duty to provide support is a rule that one only has to provide support to the land in its natural condition, not to any extra weight placed on it. This rule has resulted in many court cases fighting over whether the weight of a building caused the cave-in or whether it would have caved in even without the building. The number of cases on this issue show how difficult it is to determine what caused the cave-in. In most cases, expert engineers must be called in and the jury must decide which one is more believable.

An exception to this exception is if the excavator was negligent. If an excavator carefully shores up a building when he is excavating and it settles anyway, he is not liable. But if the owner can convince a jury that the excavator did something wrong or that he didn't do enough to shore up the building, the excavator can be held liable.

🏠 *A couple became aware that their home on the side of a mountain in Glen Ferris, West Virginia was slowly slipping down the side of the mountain. The cause of the slippage, they felt, was the failure of their neighbor to maintain a retaining wall. The retaining wall was four feet high and was entirely on the neighbor's property. It had fallen into disrepair when she bought the property. The couple spent thousands of dollars to repair their house and sued the owner for failure to provide support for their property. Their case was dismissed, but the Supreme Court of West Virginia took their appeal. It ruled that if they could prove that the land would have subsided even without the weight of their house on it, then they could collect. Otherwise they could collect nothing.*

🏠 *After buying some lots on a terraced hillside north of Hollywood Blvd. in Hollywood, California, a realty company excavated one of the lots to bring it level to that of its other lots. A few days after the work was done, the adjacent lot caved in and lost two-thirds of its area. The owner of the lot sued and was awarded damages. The court ruled that even if the person excavating his lot was not negligent, he can be held liable for damages caused by his removal or lateral support for a neighbor's land.*

🏠 *A woman sued the City of Parkersburg for trespass and sought to recover damages caused by the undermining and sloughing away of her lot and the settling of her house. She alleged it was caused by the city's collection of large quantities of rain and surface waters through its sewage system. The waters were then cast upon her property. The jury ruled in her favor.*

In this case, the appeals court reversed the decision, finding reversible error in the judge's instruction that it was the city's duty to keep storm sewers in a condition as not to permit water in them to escape and damage others' property. The court also held that a city only owes its citizens reasonable care in avoiding damage to others' property when maintaining its sewerage system. The court stated she was entitled to recover only temporary damages measured by the cost of repairs and expenses. They set aside the verdict as it was excessive. The jury considered damage to the house which it should not have done in reaching its decision.

🏠 *A couple hired a contractor and an architect to build an apartment building on property they owned on Queen Anne Hill in Seattle, Washington. The contractor was negligent in failing to brace the adjacent property and damage was caused to two adjacent buildings. The adjacent owners won a judgment against both the contractor and the couple. Because the constitution of the state of Washington requires compensation for the damaging of property, it did not matter that the couple was not negligent. They were liable as the owners who had the work done, even though the negligence was the act of an independent contractor.*

When taking action to support one's property, one must be sure to do so in a safe manner or be held liable.

🏠 *A couple lived on a sloping lot in Hawaii. To level their property, they built an eighteen-foot high retaining wall. Years later, the wall collapsed causing personal injuries and property damage to the couple who lived on the slope below them. The owners were held liable for the damages when the court ruled that a property owner has the responsibility to see that his or her retaining wall is built properly.*

Another problem related to excavating occurs when one party digs under the property of another. Since a property owner owns from the center of the earth to the heavens, any digging under the surface is a trespass and it has usually been accepted that the owner is entitled to be compensated. However, some courts have found exceptions to this rule.

🏠 *After purchasing the right to mine coal on thirty-nine acres of land in Knox County, Kentucky, a coal company caused injury to and took coal from another part of the owner's land. The landowner filed a lawsuit claiming $1,350 for injury to her land and $20,000 for coal. The company appealed, arguing, among other things, that the coal was valued too highly. The court ruled that where a person takes coal through an honest mistake, the amount of damages is the value of the royalty usually paid for the right to mine. Where a person willfully takes the coal, the damages are the value of the coal without subtracting the cost of mining.*

🏠 *In Edmonson County, Kentucky, a man discovered a cave on his land. Because it was near the world famous Mammoth Cave, he was able to operate a profitable business of providing tours and running a motel business. However, part of the cave was located under the land of*

*his neighbor. The neighbor sued for his share of the prof-
its, since the tours of the cave were trespassing onto his
land. The litigation went on for over eight years and
included four published appeals. Before it ended, the
neighbor had died and the suit had to be continued by his
administrator. In the end, his estate was awarded a por-
tion of the profits based upon the percentage of the cave
that he owned.*

Mineral Rights. In situations where mineral rights are owned by
someone other the owner of the land itself, the owner of the mineral rights has the duty to support the surface of the land and not
allow it to collapse.

It is also possible for a person to remove support from a neighbor's property without even going near it. If a person takes enough
water out of his well, the water under neighboring properties will
also be withdrawn. This can cause the neighboring properties to settle. Under the ancient principles of water law, a person could
withdraw unlimited amounts of water from his own property without liability for what might happen to his neighbors. However, this
doctrine has come into question in recent years and some courts
have begun to modify it.

If the settling of the land causes damage to structures on the
land, the person who withdrew the water (or oil) may be liable.
However, if a landowner later builds a structure on his or her land
that causes it to settle, the person who originally withdrew the water
would usually not be liable.

🏠 *Some landowners in the Seabrook and Clear Lake area of
Harris County, Texas brought action against a development and its parent company. They alleged that severe
subsidence of their lands was caused by the company's
past and continuing withdrawals of vast quantities of
underground water from their wells. The lower court
ruled for the development company, but the appeals court
reversed.*

In this case, the Texas Supreme Court reinstated the lower court's verdict, but held that from then on, the negligent withdrawing of ground water that results in subsidence of others' land would allow recovery.

In some localities, zoning laws have been passed that prohibit excavations such as quarries that cause a lot of dust, noise, and vibrations. Some of these laws have been upheld, but others have been thrown out.

🏠 *Oakland Township, Michigan, passed a law called the Conservation of Natural Resources Ordinance that required landowners to obtain permits before mining gravel or other materials. When one company applied for a permit, it was denied. The company sued and had the law declared unconstitutional. The court noted that there were no objective standards for issuing or denying a permit. The act of denying a permit in the area where there were other such pits would amount to a confiscation of the landowner's property.*

Under a federal law, *the Surface Mining Control and Reclamation Act of 1977*, some excavations for mining are required to replace the surface of the land after the mining operation has been completed.

In many states, the common law rights and duties of landowners have been modified by statutes. Some of these laws require the support of land and the buildings on it, while some require a landowner to support his own buildings. Other laws have clauses that only apply when excavations or foundations are made to certain depths.

BUSINESSES
Much of the litigation regarding businesses in residential neighborhoods has been eliminated by the practice of putting deed restrictions on property and the proliferation of zoning laws.

Today the issue of whether a business is legal in a certain location is usually very simple. Either it is allowed by zoning and restriction laws or it is not. If it is legal, there is not much that neighbors can do unless they suffer substantial injuries. If it is not legal, the business usually has few options, since invalidating deed restrictions and obtaining a zoning variance are difficult, expensive, and time consuming.

Business Next to a Residential Zone

One problem that often comes up today is that of a business legally in a business zone, next to a residence in a residential zone. The business may be producing only the normal level of noise and annoyances for its type, but that level may be too much for the residents next door.

In most cases of this type, the residence owner has few options. Only if the business is unusually obnoxious for its type and if it substantially injures the neighbor, is there a chance of winning a legal action.

🏠 *A new supermarket was built in South Carolina. The people who lived next to it sued because of the trucks unloading produce and picking up trash at night. In addition, large exhaust fans were blowing toward their homes, floodlights were shining on their home, with crowds of people and automobiles inundating the area. The court held that since the store was lawfully in a business zone, it did not have to pay for the depreciation in value of nearby residences. However, the fans and floodlights could constitute a nuisance.*

🏠 *A company located in a residential area of Nebraska City, Nebraska, decided to add meat slaughtering to its other activities. This caused noise, odors, and a host of other unpleasantries. Responding to a lawsuit filed by the neighbors, the court noted that the slaughtering caused blood and animal parts to fall all over the place and that barrels of animal parts would be left outside. This attracted numbers of dogs and flies. The court noted,*

"There were small flies and big flies, houseflies and blowflies of the most annoying and revolting kind." There were also hideous cries of anguish from the animals that apparently sensed their fates. The court also explained in detail how the animals were killed. Needless to say, the slaughterhouse was ordered to stop operations in the residential neighborhood.

Neighbors brought suit against a veterinarian in St. Louis, Missouri, when he began using his residence as a hospital for dogs and cats. The deed restrictions in the neighborhood said that the property should only be used for residences, except that physicians and dentists could have offices in their homes. The court held that a veterinarian was not a physician or dentist under the restrictions and entered an injunction forbidding the property to be used as a dog and cat hospital.

Residential Property Converting to Commercial

Another problem that can arise is where a homeowner in a residential area next to a commercial area wants to convert his property to commercial. Often his property is worth little as residential, but would be worth a lot as commercial.

The problem for the courts is that if they let that person change his property use to commercial, then the person next door will be in the same predicament. If continued, this could result in a domino effect. A related consideration is that the owner next to the commercial property would naturally have paid less for his property because of its location. By changing his use, the court would be revaluing his property at the expense of his neighbor.

For these reasons, courts have been reluctant to allow changes in use for borderline properties, whether they were limited by restrictions or zoning.

ANIMALS

The problems involved in the keeping of animals by neighbors usually relate to things such as noise, odors, health problems, and physical dangers. In most situations, there are laws and regulations that protect people from serious problems with animals. Therefore, the second approach to an animal problem with a neighbor (after approaching the owner directly) would be to contact local government agencies. In some areas, there may be specific agencies that deal with dog or animal problems. In other areas, the problems may be handled by the health, police, or other departments. If no solution is found through the owner or a government agency, then you may want to rely upon your common law rights and bring a civil suit.

Too Many Animals

Some municipalities have laws that limit the number of animals a person can keep on his or her property. These laws are usually enforceable unless they violate one of the constitutional rights discussed in Chapter 1.

> The city of Topeka once passed an ordinance that limited the number of cats or dogs a person could keep in a residence. The number was five. An attorney owned eight cats and lived with them in a large residence. The cats were born in the house and had never been allowed to leave the residence. The attorney filed suit to enjoin the police from enforcing the ordinance. The case was dismissed, but he appealed to the Supreme Court of Kansas.

In this case, the opinion written by the court included a bit of the history of cats. The judge suggested some good books on the history of cats including *The Fireside Sphinx.* He ruled that the ordinance was void because it arbitrarily limited the number of cats to five without any determination as to whether or not the cats were an actual nuisance. He ruled that the ordinance would also be void because it allowed animal hospitals to keep an unlimited number of cats, regardless of how much of a nuisance they were.

🏠 *A veterinary hospital for small animals had been operating at the same location in Columbus, Ohio for many years, when residents in the area complained to the city. The owner was charged with violating the section of the city code that stated: "No person shall keep or harbor any animal or fowl…that howls or barks or emits audible sounds to the annoyance of the inhabitants of this city." The trial court found that the hospital had been in operation for many years in a municipal zone area permitting small animal hospitals.*

In this case, the Supreme Court of Ohio dismissed the charges and added the following poem to its legal opinion.

*Dogs will howl and cats will yowl
When placed in congregation
These grating sounds may oft result
In human aggravation.
Laws passed to curb such pesky noise
Should fit the situation
And be so phrased in artful ways
To cause no obfuscation.
In other words, the laws so passed
Must plainly be effective.
Inaptly framed, they lack the force
To meet their planned objective.*

Besides ordinances, property rules and regulations may limit the number of animals. These rules may be condominium rules, deeds restrictions, or subdivision regulations.

🏠 *In Massachusetts, the Weymouthport Condominium trust bylaws were amended to forbid the keeping of any animals in the complex. A couple who later bought a unit, bought a dog. When notified that the dog violated the rules, they moved and rented out the unit, but they even-*

tually moved back in with two dogs. The condominium association fined them $5 a day and filed a court action to force them to remove the dogs. They argued that the rule and fines were invalid but both the trial and appeals courts found them valid. The fine, attorney fees, and court costs amounted to $15,244.75—not including their own attorney fees.

Diseased Animals

In rural areas, the keeping of diseased animals can be a problem for all of the surrounding neighbors as the disease can spread. For this reason, there are many laws dealing with this particular problem.

If the animals have just been brought into the state from another state, then the federal laws dealing with inspection and quarantine of animals in interstate commerce would be applicable. Several states also have rules covering the importation of animals.

For animals that have not been transported between states, there are numerous other laws that may apply. These include *bovine tuberculosis* statutes, *tick eradication* statutes, and *quarantine* statutes. In some areas the government can require owners to have their animals treated for certain diseases or even to be killed, if necessary.

NOTE: *For more information about specific remedies, contact the United States Department of Agriculture or your local state department handling similar matters.*

Cruelty to Animals

Under the common law, animals had no rights whatsoever. Being cruel to your own animals or even torturing them was not illegal. It would only have been illegal to be cruel to someone else's animal, because it was interference with that person's property.

Today, most areas have laws against cruelty to animals. These laws have been upheld as valid exercises of governmental power.

Scientific experimentation however, has usually been held to be an exception to these laws.

Enforcement of animal cruelty laws are handled by different government departments, depending on the locale. If you are bothered by a neighbor who is cruelly treating an animal, contact your local police to determine where such complaints are addressed. In some cases, it would be the police and in others it may be a special animal control department.

In most areas, there are societies for the prevention of cruelty to animals. Two of these groups are the *American Society for the Prevention of Cruelty to Animals* and the *Humane Society*. These groups will take a special interest in the problem and probably help you put an end to the situation.

Damages by Animals

Under ancient common law principles, an owner of animals (other than dogs and cats) is liable for any damages their animals do if they trespass on other people's property. This is because the owners are considered to have a duty to keep their animals locked up.

Most states in America have adopted this rule, but several western states have laws that relieve an owner of animals from liability if he or she at least makes an attempt to fence in his animals. In some states, there are laws that require people to fence their property to keep animals out. If they fail to do so, then the owners are not liable for any damage they cause. If wild animals do damage, there is usually nothing that can be done since that is considered an *act of God* or *just part of nature*. (But occasionally one can find someone to sue.)

🏠 *A farmer in Wyoming was growing a substantial crop of barley. A huge flock of ducks descended upon the area. The testimony was: "Nobody ever saw that many ducks in the sky before;" "a cloud of ducks;" "the sky was black over his field several nights;" and, "just as thick as you could see." They wiped out the part of his grain that he had not yet harvested. The farmer sent a damage claim to*

> *the Game and Fish Commission for $3,954.25 for duck*
> *depredation of his grain crop, but the Commission*
> *rejected his claim. The District Court awarded the farmer*
> *$1,113.75 for the damage to his grain and the commission*
> *appealed. The Wyoming Supreme Court affirmed, holding*
> *that there was no evidence of an abuse of discretion by*
> *the lower court.*

With domestic animals such as dogs and cats, liability depends on the local law. In some areas, there is a *one-bite rule* that says that unless an owner knows his animals are dangerous, he is not liable. Once an animal has bitten someone, it is known to be dangerous and therefore the owner is liable for any subsequent bites. However, more and more areas are rejecting the one-bite rule and holding all owners of animals liable for their actions.

> 🏠 *A farmer in Wisconsin kept his riding horses in a field*
> *adjoining a school playground. The horses were penned*
> *in by a wire fence that met the legal requirements for*
> *fences. The school children would customarily feed and*
> *pet the horses. One day, Brownie, a seven-year-old horse*
> *with no prior vicious propensities, bit an eleven-year-old*
> *girl on the ear as she was standing by the fence. The trial*
> *court held for the farmer since there was no reason for*
> *him to know of Brownie's vicious tendencies and was*
> *therefore not negligent.*

In this case, the Wisconsin Supreme Court affirmed, stating that without evidence that Brownie had previously bitten anyone, the owner was not negligent for Brownie's action. The court stated that owners of animals are only liable for damages caused by an animal due to traits of which the owner has knowledge. The court in essence allowed Brownie "one bite" and from then on, the farmer had knowledge of Brownie's tendencies.

🏠 *A young girl was walking with her father down Rainier Avenue in Seattle when a chimpanzee attacked her and mangled her right hand. In a lawsuit, the court held the owner liable. The Washington Supreme Court affirmed the judgment since the evidence showed that the owner had knowledge of the dangerous propensities of the chimp; was negligent in not leashing the animal; and, witnesses stated the girl did nothing to provoke or enrage the chimp.*

An owner of domestic animals can also be liable for injuries caused by them if he or she is in some way negligent or if the animals caused injury in an area where they should not have been allowed to go. In some areas, there are laws that overrule these common law principles and make owners of dogs liable for injuries that they cause in certain circumstances.

Dangerous Animals
When an animal is known to be dangerous, whether it is because it was dangerous in the past or because it is by nature dangerous (such as a lion), the owner is strictly liable for any injuries it causes. *Strict liability* means that the owner is liable even if he has done nothing negligent.

There are laws in some states that protect a dog owner from liability if the owner puts a *Beware of Dog* sign on his property. However, the ultimate result of a case depends on all the circumstances.

🏠 *In Florida, a couple went to a woman's home to purchase some of the products she made in her home business. The owner told them to ignore the Beware of Dog sign because the dog was secured. Unfortunately, the gate was not secured and the dog bit the wife's finger. She sued for damages. The trial court held for the owner because she had displayed a Beware of Dog sign in a prominent place on the premises. Therefore, under Florida law, she was immune from liability for damages resulting from a dog bite.*

In this case, the Appeals Court reversed the decision and held her liable. The Florida Supreme Court affirmed this decision stating that immunity would not extend to a dog owner who specifically directed a business invitee to ignore the *Beware of Dog* sign on the premises.

When a dangerous animal constitutes an annoyance to neighboring property owners, it may be ruled to be a nuisance and ordered removed from the property. For instance, in one case, a property owner who kept bee hives on his property was ordered to remove them because they stung the neighbors.

In some circumstances, persons other than the owner of an animal may be liable for injuries caused by it.

Example: In Laredo, Texas, a woman suffered a miscarriage when an elephant crashed through a concrete wall and charged into her yard. The elephant had been part of a local carnival. The court held that both the carnival and the grocery store that sponsored the carnival could be held liable.

Trespassing Animals

When an animal trespasses onto one's land, the property owner is permitted to use as much force as is reasonably necessary to drive off the animal. If an animal is vicious and liable to cause harm—it is legal to kill it. However, if it is not doing anything wrong, the property owner may not kill it in vengeance for previous trespassing.

–3–

PROBLEMS WITH
PERSONAL BEHAVIOR

At some point you will have a complaint regarding what others are doing and how it affects the enjoyment of your home. Whether they are too loud, decide to congregate on your property, or engage in activities on or near your home that displease you, you need to know what to do. This chapter instructs you as to what your rights are and how to deal with these nuisances.

NOISE

Noise can be one of the worst neighbor problems you can have. While you can forget about your neighbor's fence being over the line or his rusting truck in the front yard, a noise that keeps you from getting enough sleep or that keeps you on edge can make you physically ill. When we are not allowed the quiet we need for sleep and relaxation, it can affect many aspects of our lives including our relationships and our health.

However, not all noise that is bothersome is illegal. Courts have ruled that no one is entitled to absolute quiet in the enjoyment of his property. Some of the things that determine if a noise is allowable are the following.

◆ Is it a reasonable or unreasonable noise?
◆ Is it occurring at a reasonable or unreasonable time of day?
◆ Who was there first?

Reasonable Noise

The level of allowable noise is usually what is customary to the community. The amount of noise considered a nuisance in a quiet suburban community may be considered normal in an industrial area.

Some activities in modern society cannot be performed without noise. The courts take this into account when deciding if a noise is a nuisance. For a noise to be considered a nuisance, it must be considered "unreasonable" and annoying to a person of "ordinary sensibilities." Usually there is no exact definition of either of these terms. In most cases it will just depend on what a judge, jury, or law enforcement officer determines at the time.

In an attempt to make the laws more precise, some municipalities have defined *prohibited noise* as being *above a certain decibel level, at a certain distance.* There are electronic devices that can measure noise. These can tell you if a noise is above an allowable level.

Some areas have laws both defining a certain decibel level as being illegal and saying that noise must not be unreasonable. This makes it easier to stop an offending noise, because even if it is not above the specific limit, it can still be prohibited if a judge can be convinced that it is unreasonable for the time and place.

In some cities, the laws list certain noises that are specifically prohibited, such as car horns (except in an emergency) or dogs that bark continuously. Some states have laws limiting the noise of certain activities (transportation, industry). The federal government has the *Noise Control Act.* It is contained in Title 42, United States Code, Sections 4901 through 4918 and provides for both criminal penalties and citizen suits, and covers railroads, motor carriers, and others.

After losing cases against noisemakers, some people have tried suing over the vibration from the noise, arguing that the vibrations have *trespassed* on their property. This theory has not been successful, as courts have held that noise and vibrations are not *things* that can trespass.

In condominiums, apartments, and planned developments, noise can be easier to control because the rules are often written to forbid noise that is bothersome to other residents, even if it is *not unreason-*

able. Because these are private areas, they can limit the rights of residents much more than the government can. However, one question could be whether the rule was in effect before the offender bought his property. If so, it would clearly be enforceable. If the rule was passed later (in response to the noise), his rights would depend on whether the original restrictions or state law allows such modifications to the rules development rules.

NOTE: *A noise is not necessarily deemed a nuisance just because a person is unusually sensitive to noise and is upset by it.*

🏠 *In Brookline, Pennsylvania, there was a woman who would play her marimba on the front porch for long periods of time. She played it so loudly that it disturbed the whole neighborhood. She also would play songs intending to disturb particular neighbors. For instance, when one man entered or left his home, she would play "Jingle Bells" on the marimba because he resembled Santa Claus. She would also play "When Irish Eyes are Smiling" to annoy an Irishman, and play "Anchors Aweigh" to annoy a naval officer living in the neighborhood. An elderly woman, was always greeted with "Little Old Lady" whenever she entered or left her home.*

In this case, the court held that while playing the marimba is not generally a nuisance, because she had played it so loudly, for such long periods of time, and at unreasonable hours, it had injured her neighbors and was a nuisance. The court forbade her from playing at certain hours and strictly limited the number of hours she could play in one day. The court also forbade her from playing *Jingle Bells, When Irish Eyes Are Smiling, Anchors Aweigh,* and *Little Old Lady* with the intention of annoying and disturbing her neighbors.

Reasonable Time

Part of the requirement that noise not be unreasonable is determined by the time of day. What is a problem in the middle of the night, may be perfectly legal during the day. As one judge wrote:

"Mankind needs to sleep for a succession of several or more hours once in every twenty-four hours, and nature has provided a time for that purpose, to wit, the nighttime, and by common consent of civilized man the night is devoted to rest and sleep, and noises which would not be adjudged nuisances, under the circumstances, if made in the daytime, will be declared to be nuisances if made at night and during the hours which are usually devoted by the inhabitants of that neighborhood to sleep."

The biggest problems arise when people who need to sleep in the daytime live near neighbors who are noisy. In most cases, the law tries to balance the rights of both parties. The person making the noise, in most cases, feels he has just as much right to use his property as he wishes, as the person wanting to sleep in the daytime. The *special need* of one property owner (the sleep in the daytime) is usually not a good reason to take away the legal rights of another property owner (to use his property as he wishes).

If you have a noise problem because you need to sleep in the daytime, get an opinion from a neutral party as to whether the noise is unreasonable without considering that someone wants to sleep. As discussed earlier, there are often ways to solve a neighbor problem on your own. If simple earplugs are not enough to allow you to sleep with the noise, there are electronic noise suppression headphones that may help to shut out the noise.

A gentleman was keeping some roosters at his residence in Shreveport, Louisiana. This was not appreciated by at least two of his neighbors. A neighbor and her son claimed they were awakened each morning at five o'clock a. m. (four o'clock Standard time) by the roosters. The owner did not solve the problem. The neighbors filed a lawsuit asking for $500 in damages and for the court to order him to stop his roosters from awakening them.

However, the court did not see it their way and ruled that the crowing of a rooster at the break of day would not be a nuisance to persons of ordinary sensibilities and normal habits and tastes.

Who Was First?

If you move into a house and are disturbed by noise that had occurred long before you arrived, you will have a more difficult case than if the noise started after you moved in. This is especially true if none of the other neighbors have previously complained about the noise. (An exception would be in California where you can sue the seller if he didn't tell you about the noise.)

Generally, courts do not like to give newcomers more rights than the people who have been in an area. Exceptions are made where something is clearly unreasonable, but was never complained about before.

🏠 *In North Dakota, a woman bought the land next door to a wind generator and moved a mobile home onto it. Two years later she sued the owner of the generator claiming it was a nuisance and that it violated the restrictive covenants on the property. Even though the sound at her home was measured at a level that would be irritating and stressful, after a trial and appeal to the Supreme Court of North Dakota, she lost. The factors against her were that she moved to the claimed nuisance; waited two years before complaining; and, then only complained after her husband and the owner had gotten into some conflicts. The court also found that the restrictive covenants had been abandoned by the developer and the other residents of the subdivision.*

ANNOYING BEHAVIOR

Some behavior does not fit into any of the categories in this book, yet it is bothersome. It is not necessarily noise. It is not necessarily an odor. However, it is obnoxious.

🏠 *For three years, a lady had been doing certain things that disturbed her neighbor in Duval County, Florida. These things included operating her lawn mower in an unnecessarily noisy manner, at an early hour of the morning, close to the neighbor's bedroom; making obscene gestures toward his family; focusing a light on his residence at night; and, inciting her dog to bark boisterously to annoy him. The neighbor filed a lawsuit and was granted an injunction and damages of $500. On appeal the Supreme Court of Florida upheld the verdict, even though it was claimed that the lady was not mentally well. The ruling held that her husband was also liable for acquiescing in and condoning her conduct.*

🏠 *A couple living in Illinois began receiving numerous items through the mail that they had not ordered. These were followed by bills for the items. In a lawsuit, they alleged that their neighbor intentionally ordered these items and that such actions constituted an invasion of their privacy. The trial court dismissed their case.*

In this case, the appeals court, however, after reviewing the history of the developing law of privacy, decided that the facts alleged by them would constitute a claim for invasion of privacy that could be presented to a jury.

🏠 *An ordinance passed by the city of Hope, Arkansas, made it unlawful to construct any residence without connecting it to a sewer. One gentleman, who was building a residence, did not want to have toilet facilities in his home. He wished to equip it with toilet facilities of the out-door type and filed a suit against the city. He lost, but appealed to the Arkansas Supreme Court that held the law unconstitutional. It said that a residence was not necessarily a nuisance and that under state law, the city could not require someone who was more than 300 feet from a sewer to connect to it.*

Practical Jokes

There is nothing that can be done legally when a neighbor plays a harmless practical joke. There is no law on the books or court decision making it illegal to make a fool of someone. It is just one of the risks of living in a free society. However, where the joke causes actual harm, there are a couple of possible remedies available.

Where the joke causes some injury or damage to property, the remedy can be either criminal or a civil action for damages. Where the harm is some sort of emotional injury, recovery is not as simple, but several cases have recognized a right to recovery.

🏠 *A woman was told that her husband had been in an accident and had both legs broken, but it was not true. She suffered a shock to her nervous system and became seriously ill. A jury awarded her damages. The judgment was upheld on appeal because the defendant had willfully done an act calculated to cause physical harm, and the cause and effect of the harm was sufficiently close.*

🏠 *A woman who had been in an insane asylum twenty years earlier, lived as a successful soap saleswoman in Webster Parish, Louisiana. While traveling her route, she was told by a fortune teller that some of her relatives had buried some gold. Having heard a family tradition that a large amount of gold had been buried by her ancestors, she believed it. With the help of some relatives and friends, she began digging for the gold. After much dig-ging uncovered nothing, a neighbor came up with the idea of burying a pot of gold for them to find. They took a copper pot, filled it with rocks and dirt, and buried it with a note stating that it should not be opened for three days after it was found. When it was found, the woman planned a big celebration at a local bank for the opening of the pot and even invited a judge from a nearby town. At the opening ceremony, she was so humiliated that she flew into a rage and died within two years. Her heirs con-tinued her lawsuit against the perpetrators of the joke after her death and were awarded damages. The Supreme Court of Louisiana said that had she lived, it would have awarded her even more for her humiliation.*

Verbal Abuse

There is not much that can be done legally about verbal abuse from neighbors. In a conversation between two parties, there has rarely in history been any liability except in cases of extremely outrageous behavior that shocks the conscience and causes some physical injury to the other person.

Where a third party is present and defamatory remarks are made about one person in the presence of the other, then there may be lia-bility for slander.

Slander and Libel. Slander is when a person makes a verbal, false, and defamatory statement about a person to a third party. If the statement is written, then it is legally known as *libel.*

Truth is a defense to slander and libel. If someone calls you a crook and you have been convicted of theft, then you cannot sue for slander. But if the statement is false, it does not matter if the person making the statement thought it was true. The issue is whether the statement was actually true or false. One exception to this is if the statement was made in the form of an opinion. If a person states that in her opinion, an act is crooked, this can be considered a *privileged opinion.*

The statement must be *made to a third person*. If someone calls you a crook and no one else hears it, it is not slander. The rationale behind this is that if no one else heard it, then your reputation could not have been injured. The statement must be *defamatory*. This means that it must injure a person's reputation with a segment of the population

The statement must also be clearly about a specific person and the person defamed must be alive. (A corporation can be defamed, but a dead person can not.)

There are some exceptions to the law of slander and libel. In these situations the communication of a defamatory remark is privileged and does not subject the person making the statement to liability. The exceptions are:

- ◆ judicial proceedings. Statements made in judicial or quasi-judicial proceedings are privileged because it is in the interest of the judicial body to have everyone speak freely without fear of liability.
- ◆ legislative proceedings. Statements made by legislators in their legislative functions are privileged under the same rationale as for judicial proceedings.
- ◆ government officials. Where a defamatory statement is made by a governmental official in the course of his or her job, it is privileged for all federal officials and many state officials.
- ◆ husbands and wives. Communications between spouses are privileged because under the law they are considered one person.
- ◆ consent. If a person consents to have statements made, he or she cannot sue over them.

CROWDS

Ordinary crowds are a normal incident of city life and can be expected in places where business is conducted. However, in some cases, particularly disorderly or offensive crowds may be illegal and may be stopped by a civil action.

Criminal laws that *forbid loitering or unlawful assembly* may be useful in dispersing crowds. By contacting your local police authority, you can find out if there is anything criminal about the activity that bothers you. However, because of the constitutional right of assembly, there is a limit to how far such restrictions can go.

If it is not possible to solve the problem through police action, there may be a civil remedy. If actions of a neighbor attract a crowd that causes substantial injury to you or your property, it may be considered a nuisance.

🏠 *In 1695 (thirteen years before George Washington's mother was born), a gentleman erected a playhouse in Lincoln's Inn Fields near Portugal Row in England. This caused a problem for the residents of the row who could not get their carriages in or out of their coach-houses. This well-to-do group appealed to officers of the king. The officers prosecuted the gentleman and obtained a writ prohibiting the continuing of the inconvenience.*

🏠 *Many years later, in England, a similar commotion was caused. The store owner placed three satirical effigies in the window of his store These caused a crowd to gather that created a lot of commotion on the street annoying neighboring shopkeepers. In a court action in 1830, this was held to be a nuisance. During the store owner's trial, a story was told of another gentleman whose daughter worked for him in his shop. His daughter was so beautiful, that every day three to four hundred people would gather in the street to look at her. Eventually she had to be sent out of town.*

🏠 *In New York, in the 1880s, a couple whose extraordinary long hair was a museum attraction, used their bay window to comb their hair and to promote their hair tonic. This attracted a crowd that blocked the entrance to a business in the basement of the building. The court ordered the pair to stop causing such a crowd.*

🏠 *A restaurant in Detroit, Michigan must have had fantastic food in the 1940s. Crowds would gather, blocking neighboring stores. The crowds were so big that the stores' window displays were almost completely blocked from view. The restaurant was ordered to hire a guard to supervise the lines.*

🏠 *Americans in the 1940s seem to have been in a feeding frenzy. Later that decade, in West Palm Beach, Florida, Morrison's Cafeteria was the place to eat. It was so popular that lines would form out the front door. The lines became so long that they blocked the entrance to a neighboring drug store. In a court action by the drug store, a court ordered Morrison's to put an end to the lines.*

🏠 *When an Italian Pub in Fort Wayne, Indiana was in danger of losing its liquor license, it told the liquor control commission that it was hiring a police officer to maintain order in the neighborhood. It also passed out flyers in the neighborhood offering to help if there was a disturbance in the neighborhood. When a person was assaulted in a parking lot across the street from the pub on a day when the policeman was late for work, a court held that the pub could be held liable for the injury if a jury decided that that the pub assumed the duty of protecting the neighborhood.*

But not all judges have been sympathetic with neighbors who object to crowds. In some cases it has been held that if a person is carrying on a lawful business and a crowd gathers, it is not the business person's fault.

🏠 *After World War II, potatoes were in short supply in England and were being rationed. One shopkeeper obtained a supply and a line formed to his shop, blocking several other shops. In this case, the court held that the shopkeeper was not responsible for the short supply of potatoes and would not be liable for the crowds.*

🏠 *The Taft Stadium Board of Control began allowing midget auto racing in Taft Stadium in Oklahoma City. A neighbor who lived a block and a half from the stadium was not pleased with the races. He filed suit complaining that cars parked in the area; crowded the streets; blocked driveways; and, made it impossible for two cars to pass on the streets. He also complained about the noise and devaluation of property values.*

In this case, the court ruled for the stadium authority quoting other cases that held—

City streets are primarily ways for public travel, and public right of travel includes privilege of parking vehicles at sidewalk curbing for reasonable periods as required by reasonable exigencies of business or social intercourse, "and "these are the plagues of city dwellers.

STREET GANGS

In some cities, gang activity has caused problems for neighbors. In some, the police can handle it adequately, in others it is out of control. Some neighborhoods form committees to patrol their streets. In some neighborhoods these committees have been successful, but others have ended up with members being killed and their homes burned down.

The first step is always to contact your local police agency. If they can't help, you should bring it to the attention of the city administration and the media. Perhaps the local television station would film the activity for an expose.

For information on combating gang activity, including state laws relating to it, go to the web address for the *Institute for Intergovernmental Research:*

www.iir.com/nycg/gang-legis

IMMORAL ACTIVITIES

What one person considers immoral, another may consider to be the meaning of life. But when the government is concerned, many activities are decided to be immoral. Once they are deemed immoral, they can be stopped.

There are numerous specific laws making nudity, prostitution, gambling, drug sales, and the like illegal. There are also zoning laws that ban certain activities in certain areas. But citizens have also been successful in using civil lawsuits to rid their neighborhoods of offensive activities.

Disorderly houses and *bawdy houses* are two types of activities that have often been ruled to be nuisances. Bawdy houses are, in fact, considered nuisances at all times and in all places. Slaughterhouses, rendering plants, and chemical factories can be nuisances in certain cases. Disorderly houses that are gambling houses are considered nuisances per se, but other types of disorderly houses, such as saloons are only considered nuisances when they annoy the neighborhood.

> *A couple owned a group of flats in St. Louis, Missouri. Their neighbors were twenty-four different social clubs that operated a bowling alley. In addition to causing great noise, the members of the clubs exposed themselves from the open windows of the shower rooms and used loud, boisterous, and obscene language. The couple sued and the case dragged on into hundreds of pages of pleadings and testimony. In the end, the courts balanced the interests of the parties and held that the clubs must reduce their noise, stop exposing themselves, and stop using obscene language.*

🏠 *The prosecuting attorney in Seattle, Washington filed a case to close down a hotel for six months and to sell the contents. He claimed three acts of prostitution and four offers to commit prostitution were committed on the premises.*

The hotel actually had a reputation as being decent, orderly, and had respectable, permanent residents renting 80 of the 114 rooms. The bellmen involved in the alleged crimes were immediately fired. The owners had nothing to do with their actions. A local judge dismissed the case, but the prosecutor appealed to the Washington Supreme Court. That court also agreed the case should be dismissed.

🏠 *The owners of a bar in Anderson, South Carolina were convicted of the crime of operating a disorderly house. They appealed to the Supreme Court of South Carolina. Unfortunately for them, the court agreed with the trial judge that although dancing is usually an innocent amusement and drinking may also be legal, dancing and drinking accompanied by swearing, drunkenness, and annoying the neighborhood with loud and disturbing noises was a nuisance.*

PRIVACY

In most states, there are four types of invasion of privacy recognized by the law. Two of them, using someone's likeness for commercial purposes and placing someone in a false light in the public eye, usually do not apply to neighbor relations. These usually involve businesses or the news media.

The two types of invasion of privacy that may come up between neighbors are the right not to have one's solitude or seclusion intruded upon and the right not to have one's private facts disclosed. In some states, such as New York, these rights are spelled out in the statutes, but in other states, such as New Jersey, they are part of the common law developed by judges.

Peeping Tom

One type of invasion of privacy may be someone coming up to your window and peeking in or looking across from another window with a telescope. For these situations, the best solution is not a legal one— it is keeping one's curtains closed. In some states, there are laws against *window-peeping*, but there are also laws against indecent exposure. If you complain about a person watching you undress, they may charge you with exposing yourself in an open window.

As for suing someone in civil court for peeping in one's window; privacy rights are a growing area of the law. Rights that were rejected years ago are now being recognized. The time may be right for a court to award damages in such a case. However, no record has been found of any court doing so thus far. In fact, even some laws against window peeping have been thrown out.

> *A man filed a workman's compensation claim and his employer hired a private detective to investigate whether he was really injured. They followed him around, peeped in his windows, and watched him with binoculars. The man sued and the court held that since the agency had a legitimate right to investigate a claim, he could not collect unless the detectives violated a specific law while investigating him.*

Entering the Premises

When a person invades your privacy by coming onto your property or into your house, there is a much better case for recovery. The reason is there is also a trespass that is a much more easily recognized wrong. If the person touches you at the same time, that makes it an even stronger case, since it involves battery. However, in some situations, a person such as a landlord or repairman, may have a right to enter your home.

A woman in New York sued her landlord for invasion of privacy for entering her apartment and taking pictures. The court held that in New York no common law right of privacy exists and the only privacy rights are provided by statute. The New York statute on privacy only concerns the commercial exploitation of one's personality.

Disclosing Private Facts

People with whom we live in close proximity often become acquainted with intimate details of our lives. A person can be held liable for disclosure of these details if the following conditions are met:

◆ details are private or secret facts;
◆ disclosure is a public; and,
◆ making the disclosure would be offensive to a reasonable person.

One limitation to this is that persons who are in the public eye, such as movie stars, politicians, directors of organizations, and others in positions of authority, have less of a right to privacy. This is because they are considered to have placed themselves in the public eye, and in many cases, details about them are of necessary concern to the public.

When one leaves another in charge of one's property, for example, by renting it out, then that person has a right to permit others to make it public.

A couple left the country and rented their home in Georgia to another couple. While the property was rented, the tenants allowed a company to film four television commercials on the premises. The owners sued, claiming, among other things, that such filming on their premises was an invasion of their privacy. They lost. The courts held that by leasing their house, they gave up any expectation of privacy. The filming of a commercial in

*their home was not an intrusion of their seclusion, soli-
tude, or of their private affairs. They asked the appeals
court for a second hearing, and asked the Supreme Court
of Georgia to hear their case, but were denied in both
instances.*

PERSONAL INJURY

The subject of personal injuries caused either by intentional acts or
negligence is beyond the scope of this book. However, since neighbors occasionally do injure or even kill each other, a brief
explanation of the law in these areas is included.

Intentional acts such as assault and battery and *negligent acts* such
as nuisance and trespass are part of the body of law called *tort law*.
Torts are wrongful acts. Whether they are intentional or negligent,
the law allows victims of wrongful acts to receive compensation.

Threats

A mere threat is not usually something that the law offers protection for. One kind of threat that is a crime is an *assault*. An assault
is an act of putting a person in fear of receiving a battery. Common
examples of assaults would be pointing a gun at someone, driving a
car toward someone and missing him or her, or raising your fist as if
to hit someone.

> ***Example:*** In New Hampshire, two men got into an argument
> and one pointed an unloaded gun at the other. The
> one who pointed the gun was successfully sued for
> assault since pointing a gun at someone would put
> that person in fear of receiving a battery.

Intentional Injuries

Intentional acts that cause injury range from battery to murder.
Battery is any case where one person causes the touching of another
person without permission. The touching may be a tap with the

hand, shooting them with a bullet, or running over them with a car. Any unauthorized touching is considered a battery. Committing a battery can result in both a court action for damages by the person touched and a criminal charge, since battery is both a tort and a crime.

Murder is, of course, the unauthorized killing of another human. Murder would not include killing someone in self-defense, in a war, as a law enforcement officer in the line of duty, or as an agent of the state carrying out an execution.

Unintentional Injuries

Whether or not a person is liable for unintentionally injuring someone depends upon whether or not the accident was due to negligence and whether the injury was caused by some inherently dangerous activity. If it was neither of these, it may have been an *unavoidable accident* for which no one is liable.

Unavoidable Accidents

If an accident is judged to be *unavoidable*, the general rule has been that the person who caused it, is usually not liable for any injuries resulting from it, unless they were engaged in a dangerous activity. However, this rule has changed over the years. People are being held liable for accidents that formerly would have been called unavoidable. This is especially true when they have insurance.

Negligence

If an accident is caused by negligence, then the negligent person (and others such as his employer or partner) can be held liable for an injury caused by the negligence. Negligence is a subject that depends upon numerous complicated principles of law. But the ultimate decision as to whether a person is negligent depends upon whether he was using the proper amount of care under the circumstances and whether his act was the actual cause of the damages.

One of the issues that must be decided when claiming a person was negligent is what the *standard of care* was for the circumstances. This is because the law has developed different standards for different situations.

> In the 1920s, a lady was standing on the platform of the Long Island railroad waiting to go to Rockaway Beach. Another passenger was running to catch his moving train, when he started to fall. Two train guards helped him onto the train, but in doing so, caused him to drop a package he was carrying. The package, wrapped in newspaper, contained fireworks that exploded when they landed on the tracks. The shock of the explosion knocked down some scales at the other end of the platform hitting the lady. She sued the railroad and won. Her verdict was upheld by the appeals court, but the railroad appealed.

In this case, the New York Supreme Court threw out her verdict. It stated that any negligence in helping one passenger should not make one liable to another passenger at the other end of the platform from a package that did not appear dangerous.

–4–
PROBLEMS WITH BOUNDARIES

Property is a symbol of status, comfort, and security. Identifying and defining your property can often be a source of heated dispute. Neighbors trying to build a fence on your side of the property line or allowing their trees to grow over your driveway are just two examples of problems you may encounter regarding boundary lines. Issues concerning sharing a common wall are also frequent. This chapter tells you what to do to resolve these disputes.

BOUNDARY DISPUTES

Because of the difficulties in accurately measuring land, there are frequent instances where neighbors disagree about the location of property *boundaries*. Because maps are flat and the earth is curved, paper descriptions do not always match the actual shape of the land. The problems are understandable as many descriptions are based upon government surveys up to two hundred years old.

When two parties cannot locate the boundary between their property, the first step should be to have a survey done of the two *parcels*. Occasionally, a survey cannot determine the exact location of a boundary because the descriptions conflict. If this is the case, the best solution is for the parties to mutually agree on a location of the boundary.

Of course, each party would rather have his parcel as large as possible and it may be difficult to come to an agreement, especially when each person's deed seems to give him the larger piece. However, considering the cost of going to court to determine a boundary, the reward for winning may not be as great as the cost.

Some less expensive alternatives to going to court would be either *arbitration* or *mediation*. Arbitration means turning the question over to a disinterested arbitrator who would make a decision without the delay or expense of the court system. Mediation means having a trained mediator work with the parties to help them arrive at a fair resolution.

If two neighbors do arrive at an agreement as to their boundary, they should have their agreement put in writing. They should then execute deeds clearing up any questions in the title. The usual way to do this is to have the proper legal descriptions drafted by a surveyor and then to have each owner *quit claim* any interest he may have in the other property.

If the parties cannot agree on a solution or an alternative to litigation, they can have a judge and jury determine the rights to the disputed property. Many such disputes have been heard over the years. The courts have developed numerous rules to guide them in such decisions. Some of those rules are the following.

- ◆ The important consideration is the intent of the parties who divided the lands.
- ◆ If there is an ambiguity, then it is to be resolved in favor of the person who *received* the ambiguous deed, rather than the one who *conveyed* the property with the ambiguous deed.
- ◆ Where the terms of the description conflict, the court uses a *hierarchy* to determine which descriptions are controlling. That hierarchy is as follows:
  - ◆ monuments;
  - ◆ clearly marked neighbor's boundary;
  - ◆ a plat or a map prepared from a survey;
  - ◆ angles and distances of the description (angles are given preference over distances); and,
  - ◆ area measurement.

Example: If a description states that a person owns a piece of land comprising of forty acres, bounded by four corner markers and the land surrounded by those markers is only thirty-five acres, then a court will probably determine that the person only owns thirty-five acres. The corner markers will be considered to be more accurate than the measurement of the area. (However, if the person was lead to believe that he was buying forty acres, he may be able to sue the seller for misrepresentation.)

🏠 *Two neighboring ranchers in Park County, Wyoming got into a disagreement over the boundary between their ranches. One felt that the boundary should be based upon a call to a river that had been described in the original 1883 field notes of the surveyor. The other rancher felt that the boundary should be 660 feet further. The trial court ruled it was 660 feet further and the other neighbor filed an appeal with the Wyoming Supreme Court without using an attorney. The court noted that if the river was used as a monument, all three of the calls of the description would be off. If it was assumed that the river had shifted over 100 years, then only one call would need to be corrected. It also noted that if it used the river as a monument, many neighboring property descriptions would be changed. It affirmed the trial court's decision.*

🏠 *The marker for the quarter corner between land owned by the United States Government and a private couple was lost. The parties could not agree where their boundary was. The United States claimed that it should be reestablished by measurement (giving the government more land) and the couple claimed that there was enough evidence to establish where the original corner had been. A lawsuit by the United States was dismissed after the couple presented testimony of a longtime resident that a well-worn path, a post, a rock pile, a fence, and bearing trees indicated the location of the corner.*

Bodies of Water

It is possible that if your property is next to a nonnavigable body of water (lake, pond, or small river), the legal description describing your property will use the body of water to identify what you own. In a situation such as this, if the person conveying the property owns to the center of the body of water, it is assumed that the conveyance includes to the center of the body of water and that the seller did not intend to keep a strip of land underwater. This is also true where a road is used in the description. A legal description that describes the property as *running to a road* will include to the center of that road, if the person conveying the land owned to the center of the road.

NOTE: *This does not apply to governmental units that convey property.*

> **Example:** A town in Vermont denied a homeowner a permit to keep a trailer on his lot because the lot was not large enough. The town failed to consider the underwater land up to the middle of the channel, owned by the homeowner. The court said that this was an error and that the underwater land should be included in calculating the size of his lot.

In some areas, local authorities have passed laws forbidding property to be divided without compliance with numerous governmental requirements.

> **Example:** Island County, Washington and the State of Washington once filed suit against a developer who allegedly subdivided land improperly. The Supreme Court of Washington affirmed the dismissal of the complaint on the ground that the submerged land to the center of the lake could be included in the size of the lots to make them five acres in size and exempt from the platting requirement.

Where a boundary is marked by a river, stream, or other body of water, a change in the location of the waterway can change the boundary of the property. This is an ancient rule of property law. However, over the years, exceptions to the rule have been allowed, especially when sticking to the rule would have been unfair.

One modern rule is that when a river slowly changes its course, the property line changes with it. However, when it suddenly changes its course, the boundary line remains where it originally was.

🏠 *A dispute arose between a landowner in Oregon and the United States government because of a conveyance in 1887 to the U.S. of land to be used as a life saving station. The land was on the Columbia River. The government no longer used the land for life saving and the landowner brought a quiet title action. The District Court held that the government did not have title to the land, but that the government did have an easement regardless of the fact that the walkway on the easement was being used for marine studies instead of as a life saving station. The court gave the owner title, but reserved the easement for the government to gain access to the river.*

🏠 *When a person bought a piece of land in Missouri, he received a deed that gave him all land east of Sin-A-Bar Creek. However, the creek was not in the quarter of land that he purchased, so he assumed that he owned the entire east half of it and began farming it. There was a dry creek bed on the land. A neighbor and his predecessors had been farming the land east of the creek bed for many years. The neighbor sued to regain possession of the land. The new buyer claimed that the creek was a monument on his deed and it had moved. Therefore, he was entitled to the land east of the new location. The court looked at aerial photographs of the area and all of the deeds in the chain of title. It concluded that since the land between the channels remained unaltered, the location of the stream must have changed avulsively (through land erosion) and therefore would not have changed ownership of the land. It also noted that since the neighbor and his predecessors had farmed the land and paid taxes on it for many years, they would have owned it by adverse possession anyway.*

Party Walls

A *party wall* is a wall on the boundary line of two properties that is used by both owners. Each party owns half the wall and has an easement on the other half of the wall. The wall is usually placed equally on each side of the property line.

Party walls have been used since ancient times. They are typically found in large cities and areas where row houses are common. The use of a party wall between two properties saves the cost of building a separate wall for each building. Walls can become party walls by agreement between the parties, by statute, or by continued use.

In some areas, statutes have been passed that define the circumstances under which a wall becomes a party wall. In other areas, landowners can create a party wall by written or oral agreement or by using a wall as a party wall without any agreement or understanding. A party wall can also be created if a person owning a large piece of property deeds parts of it to two different persons and the dividing line between the parts of the property is a wall. Once a wall legally becomes a party wall, *party wall law* controls how it may be used and what the rights of the parties are. A wall remains a party wall until the two owners agree that it shall no longer be a party wall or until it decays or is destroyed. Neither owner has the right to destroy the wall without the other's consent. (A destroyed party wall can be revived by rebuilding it.)

A person building a party wall must make it strong enough to hold up buildings on both sides. There is no right to put windows in a party wall. It is legal to build chimney flues in a party wall, but if they are located on both sides of the property line, then both owners can use them. It is legal to put a sign on one's own side of a party wall, but it is not legal to put one on the other person's side.

Nothing may be built that projects over the other owner's side of the party wall. In many areas, it is legal to extend and thicken a party wall or to replace it with a better wall. However, it is not legal to make it thinner. In some states, owners are required to contribute to the cost of building a party wall.

🏠 *One person began to extend a party wall between his property and that of his neighbor in Washington, D. C. The neighbor filed suit in federal court for damages to his property and to stop the building. In examining the law of the District of Columbia, the court found that the rules for construction of party walls were issued by George Washington and were still in force. One rule allowed a property owner to build a party wall extending onto his neighbor's land.*

🏠 *Two couples were owners of adjacent parcels of land in Allentown, Pennsylvania. Each owned one-half of a double home on the properties. The home was constructed in the 1930s and contained a party wall separating the two residences. In 1979, one couple made some improvements to their property, including replacement of part of the party wall with a fire wall. The other couple filed a suit against them asking that the court order the fire wall removed since it encroached several inches onto the other property and caused water problems in the basement. The court decided that removal of the wall would do no good to the couple suing and would be a hardship on the neighbors.*

🏠 *A private property owner and Montcalm County, Michigan, owned adjoining buildings that shared a common wall until a fire destroyed the private owner's building. An engineer recommended to him that the party wall was unsound and that it should be demolished. The county refused to agree since the wall was providing some support to its roof. He sued for damages resulting from the delay in rebuilding caused by the county's refusal to remove the damaged wall. The trial court dismissed his action.*

In this case, the appeals court held that an owner of an easement right in a party wall had no obligation to agree to destroying the wall. It also held that as long as the wall provided some support to the defendant's building, the plaintiff had no right to destroy the wall and was under a duty to refrain from doing so.

🏠 *The city of La Crosse, Wisconsin brought a suit against the owner of a dilapidated building to order it be razed. It also joined the owner of the building next door that shared a party wall with the condemned building, asking the court to order him to pay the cost of strengthening the wall. The court noted that some states disagree, but that in Wisconsin, the owner of a building sharing a party wall must pay for the support of the wall.*

FENCES

Even the lowly fence can cause innumerable problems between neighbors. It can be too high, too short, too ugly, in the wrong place, or too dangerous. There can even be a problem if a person doesn't put up a fence at all. Under basic principles of law, every property owner has a *right* to build a fence around his property, but no property owner has a *duty* to build a fence. However, there are numerous exceptions to this basic rule.

The most common exception is where there is a statute or ordinance requiring or controlling fences. In both rural and urban areas, governmental bodies have found it necessary to regulate fences. In rural areas, the perceived need is to keep grazing animals confined. In urban areas, the perceived need can range from safety to aesthetics.

Rural Areas

In some states, the laws allow for fencing districts and even fence boards. These groups make decisions on location and payment for needed fences. The idea is to fairly apportion the cost of keeping all the ranches or farms fenced. The districts often levy a tax or assessment on the different owners to pay for the fences. People who fail to pay the assessment can lose their property in foreclosure.

Some areas have *fence viewers*. These are people who go out to the land and decide which landowner is responsible for building or repairing certain parts of a fence. Fence viewers may be elected or appointed and they must take an oath of office. When landowners in these areas have a dispute over a fence, they can take their problem to the local *fence viewer* for a decision.

When the fence between two properties in Chelsea, Massachusetts deteriorated, the fence viewers of Chelsea were called in. At a hearing, the fence viewers decided that the fence was "shaky, rotted away in many places, loose, improperly anchored to the ground, and lacked stability against wind pressure creating a potential hazard." The fence viewers decided that the two owners should each tear down half the fence and build a new one within thirty days. One of the owners filed suit. The local court disagreed with her, so she appealed to the Supreme Court of Massachusetts. After reviewing the Massachusetts statute and constitutional principles, the court decided that none of her rights had been violated.

In some areas the fence laws make clear what kind of fence is suitable and legal. Where there are no specifications in the law, a fence must be strong enough to turn away ordinary livestock.

> **Example:** In New Hampshire, a farmer had several cows and a bull that was especially strong and aggressive. The bull broke through the fence and the cattle destroyed some of he other farmer's hay and corn. The court ruled that even though the bull was considered a "fence breaker," the farmer was not liable for the damage because he did not legally have to make an impassible fence—only one strong enough to stop ordinary cattle.

Where fences are required by law, they may be placed equally on the land of adjoining owners. This is also true in areas where zigzag fences, such as Virginia fences or worm fences are the custom. However, where more than half of a fence is built on one person's land without his consent, he is entitled to relief.

🏠 *Two adjacent landowners in Michigan got into a controversy over their property line. One of them called out the fence viewers to decide who was responsible for the fence. It was decided that one of the landowners had to build a fence. That landowner then built a stump fence, one composed of tree stumps lying with the stump on his side and the trunk on the neighbor's side. The stump fence took up a strip of land five by five and a half foot wide. Most of the way, two thirds or more of the fence was on the neighbor's property. The neighbor sued and the trial court ruled that this was not illegal. The neighbor appealed to the Michigan Supreme Court and it ruled that the fence must be equally on each side of the boundary line.*

In some areas a person may be liable for *triple damages* or even *punitive damages* for destroying a person's fence.

> Two adjacent landowners in South Dakota got into an argument at an American Legion Club trapshoot. One of them went home and destroyed 165 feet of the neighbor's fence with his tractor. The neighbor repaired the fence and was awarded triple the cost of the repair plus $7,000 in punitive damages.

Owners of Livestock

Even if there is no law requiring a fence, owners of livestock are required to keep their animals on their property. Therefore, persons raising animals on their land may be required to build fences to keep them in. Where there is some requirement to build a fence, a person failing to do so can be liable for injuries caused by his failure to do so.

Example: Two adjacent landowners in Texas had an agreement as to which parts of the fence between their properties each was going to maintain. One of them failed to keep his section in repair and his cattle trespassed onto the other's land, causing damage to his crops. He sued and won.

Urban Areas

Fence laws are much more complicated in urban than in rural areas. There are often regulations as to height, composition, and location. In some areas, fences may even be forbidden. These rules may be contained in either local ordinances or in property restrictions.

Dangerous Fences

Whether a person is liable for injury caused by a dangerous fence is determined by the law relating to negligence. Under general principles of negligence law, a person is required to warn guests of any known dangerous conditions and is required to provide safe conditions for business visitors on the property. However, a property owner is not required to warn trespassers of unsafe conditions.

A fence may be dangerous if it is built along a well-traveled road without warnings being posted. The owner may then be liable for injuries to any travelers.

> *Example:* A landowner in California had a poorly designed and badly maintained barbed wire fence. He was later held liable when some neighboring horses were injured by the fence.

TREES AND PLANTS

Plants have been one of the earliest sources of disagreements between neighbors. Trees have fallen on people and their homes; they have blocked sunlight; they have clogged drains with their leaves; and, their roots have damaged all types of structures.

The problems encountered with plants usually fall into one of three areas:
♦ ownership;
♦ bothersome; and,
♦ danger.

Ownership

The ownership of a plant depends upon where its trunk is situated. The owner of the land where a plant is growing is the owner of the plant. The property owner also is the owner of all the fruit growing on it, even if the fruit is hanging in another person's yard.

🏠 *A woman was picking cherries from branches of her brother's cherry tree. When she attempted to pick cherries from a branch that hung over onto the neighbor's yard, the neighbor told her to stop. When she continued to pick cherries, he stopped her by using force—causing personal injury. She sued him for assault and battery. The court held that a person upon whose lands a tree wholly stands is the owner of the whole tree and is entitled to all its fruit, even if some of its branches overhang the lands of another. He was therefore liable for assault and battery.*

🏠 *Two neighbors agreed to plant hedges on the boundary line of their adjoining property at equal cost to each. Later, one cut down some of the hedges and the other brought a court action. The neighbor suing claimed they had agreed to plant on the boundary line, but did not know if this had been done. The other claimed the trees were wholly on his land. A survey showed the trees were wholly on his land. The court held that the neighbor could sue breach of the agreement to plant on the boundary line, but not for trespass and diminution of property value. The court awarded damages in the amount of his interest in the value of the trees.*

Where a plant is located directly upon a property line, it is jointly owned by both of the property owners. Each would also own any fruit of the plant. Neither one has the right to cut it down without the permission of the other. Only if the plant becomes a nuisance will the courts allow removal.

🏠 *A row of large cottonwood trees sat on the boundary line between the properties owned by two neighbors in Iowa. One of them needed the trees for protection from winter winds. The other wanted them removed because they shaded his field and made it unproductive. The court held that the damage was insufficient to warrant the trees' removal.*

Bothersome Plants and Trees

On the issue of what the remedy is for plants that are bothersome, such as trees that fill gutters with their leaves or send roots under neighbors driveways, the courts are divided into four camps. The different rules they follow are called the *Massachusetts Rule*, the *Restatement Rule*, the *Hawaii Rule*, and the *Virginia Rule*.

The Massachusetts Rule states that people who are bothered by encroaching roots and branches can cut them off at the property line themselves and should not be bringing such cases to court. The rationale is that tree growth is natural and the common sense solution is to just cut them.

The Restatement Rule is so named because it is contained in the *Restatement of Torts 2d* promulgated by the American Law Institute. This is an academic study of what the state of the law is. Under this rule, the Massachusetts approach only applies to *natural growth*. If there is some damage due to an artificial condition created on the land, such as trees planted by the owner or former owner, then the landowner can be held liable and the case may be taken to court.

The Hawaiian court rejected both the Massachusetts Rule and the Restatement Rule and made its own rule that has been adopted by several states. This court felt that the Massachusetts Rule was *simple and certain*, but that it was not realistic and fair. The *Hawaii Rule* states that when overhanging branches or protruding roots actually cause danger or there is immanent danger of them causing harm to property other than plant life, then the endangered neighbor may require the owner to cut back the plant. If the owner refuses and there is imminent danger, one can have them cut and bill the neighbor. Also, one can always cut the branches to the property line at one's own cost.

The Virginia Rule is that homeowners can only be brought to court for plants that are noxious and cause harm. The difficult issue under this rule is how to decide what is noxious.

Not all states have had a chance to issue court opinions on tree branches. So it is not known, for sure, how a similar case would be decided in all states. However, the following is a list of some states whose positions are known.

The following states appear to follow *The Massachusetts Rule.*

- Alabama
- Connecticut
- District of Columbia
- Florida
- Illinois
- Iowa
- Kentucky
- Maryland
- Massachusetts
- Nebraska
- New Jersey
- Rhode Island
- Vermont

These states seem to follow *The Restatement Rule.*

- California
- Louisiana
- Mississippi
- Missouri
- North Carolina

These states follow *The Hawaii Rule.*

- Hawaii
- Indiana
- Kansas
- Michigan
- New Mexico
- New York

◆ Ohio

◆ Oklahoma

◆ Tennessee

Arizona and Virginia are the only two states that follow *The Virginia Rule.*

The following are some noteworthy neighborhood battles over trees.

> 🏠 *When a man built a concrete patio in his yard in Suffolk County, New York, a tree belonging to his neighbor, that was near the property line and just eight or nine inches from the edge of the patio, was just three inches in diameter. Eight years later, the tree was much bigger and its roots were causing damage to the patio. When he complained to the neighbor, she told him he could remove the tree. Instead he sued her for trespass and nuisance for $1500 damage to his patio.*

In this case, the court made and exception to the self-help rule since the tree was planted before the patio was built. A previous New York case had ruled that an owner does not have to resort to self-help remedies for problems involving roots. The owner of the tree had not done anything intentional or negligent to cause the problem.

> 🏠 *In Idaho, roots from a neighbor's tree were causing a woman's basement wall to crack and cave in. She sued the neighbor and the court ruled that she could remove the neighbor's tree at her expense since it was damaging her property and therefore was a nuisance.*

> 🏠 *When roots from his neighbor's 40-year-old Monterey pine tree entered his yard and began breaking up his sidewalk, a California homeowner hired a contractor to*

excavate his yard to a depth of three feet and remove all roots. This caused the tree to die and become dangerous. His neighbor, who happened to be a lawyer, had to pay to have the tree removed. Needless to say, the lawyer sued, but the trial court ruled that a property owner has the absolute right to cut roots entering his property.

In this case, the appeals court had a much more limited view of the property owners' rights. It found that a property owner's right to cut encroaching branches and roots is limited by what is reasonable and that a property owner cannot do whatever he wishes, disregarding the rights of others.

Dangerous Plants and Trees

In cases of dangerous trees, the courts have made a distinction between rural and urban areas. In urban areas, persons in possession of land (owners or tenants) have been held to have a greater duty to inspect their trees and to be sure that they do not present a danger. However, some courts have held that if there was no reasonable way the owner would have known that the tree was defective, he would not be liable.

A man in Fultonville, New York was working on his truck in the driveway of his parent's home during a heavy windstorm. About noon, a limb from a maple tree on the neighboring property fell and severely injured him. However, his suit was dismissed because no evidence was presented that indicated that there was any evidence that the tree was defective before the accident. The court ruled that in order to collect, the injured party would have to prove that the tree was in a dangerous condition; that the condition caused the injury; that the landowner realized or should have realized that the tree was dangerous; and, that there would have been enough time to correct the danger after the landowner realized it.

In this case, the injured neighbor was not happy with this result, so he appealed to the New York Supreme Court. He lost again and asked for a second chance to argue the case before the court. This was denied. He then tried to appeal to the U. S. Supreme Court and was denied a hearing.

In some areas, local laws may make homeowners liable for injuries caused by their trees even if they were not negligent. In these areas, you need to be sure your trees are safe or keep adequate insurance to cover tree problems.

In rural areas, especially where property is owned in vast tracts of land, many courts have held that they do not have to inspect the trees and do not even have to remove, they are known to be rotten.

–5–
PROBLEMS WITH THE EARTH AND SKY

People buy property for a variety of reasons. If it is a home, one of the reasons is because you enjoy its location. If it is a farm, it may be because you need to use the water from a nearby river for irrigation. Whatever the reason, when your enjoyment changes, you want to act to prevent or correct the actions of others.

This chapter explores some of the common problems land owners face dealing with water rights. This includes drainage issues and using common sources of water; the right to light and clean air; and, some new concerns over electronic waves and radioactive contamination.

WATER

The right to water and to protection from water have caused problems between neighbors for thousands of years. And while some distinct rules have been developed, the different states in this country have not agreed as to which are the right rules for dealing with these sorts of problems.

The problems regarding water fall into three main categories:
- ◆ drainage problems with surface waters;
- ◆ rights to water in watercourses and bodies of water; and,
- ◆ rights to underground water.

Drainage Problems

Water that falls as rain or washes across property in undefined streams is called *diffuse surface water*. There are three legal doctrines recognized by different states regarding diffuse surface water. Some of the states consider this water as a *common enemy* and give the property owner the right to dam it or deflect it in any way onto other properties. Other states hold that a property owner does not have the right to obstruct the *natural flow* of the water. A more modern approach has been to allow a landowner to make *reasonable use* of diffused surface water.

Watercourses and Bodies of Water

For rights regarding watercourses and bodies of water (commonly known as rivers, lakes, ponds) the states are divided into two camps. Most of the states subscribe to the doctrine of *riparian rights*, but seventeen western states have evolved a theory of "prior appropriation." The riparian rights states are further divided into those which prefer natural flow and those which allow reasonable use.

Basically, the *riparian rights doctrine* holds that persons who own land on which there is water have the right to use the water for domestic and commercial purposes as well as for boating, swimming, and fishing. They have the rights in the quality, quantity, and the velocity of the water.

The natural flow doctrine was developed in England and holds that a riparian owner may use water, but must return it to the stream or lake in substantially the same quality and quantity. In America, most courts follow the reasonable use doctrine which allows a person to make use of the water as long as his use does not interfere with the needs of the other riparian owners.

The prior appropriation doctrine was developed in the western states of America. This doctrine holds that whoever begins making use of the water first has a right to continue that use. The rationale for this is that it encourages the development of water uses. It began with the needs of miners and farmers to divert water for long distances. Without this doctrine, people might not make the investment necessary in such arid regions.

The states which subscribe solely to the prior appropriation doctrine are Arizona, Colorado, Idaho, Montana, Nevada, New Mexico, Utah, and Wyoming. California, Texas and several other western states have combined the prior appropriation doctrine with the reasonable use doctrine.

An example of the prior appropriation rule involved Mono Lake, the second largest lake in California, which sits at the base of the Sierra Nevada escarpment near the Yosemite National Park entrance. The lake was home to vast numbers of nesting and migratory birds who lived on islands in the lake. Mono Lake received most of its water supply from five streams carrying the snowmelt of the Sierra Nevada to its shores.

The Water Department of Los Angeles appropriated virtually the entire flow of four of the five streams into aqueducts for the use of the citizens of L.A. This caused the level of the lake to drop. One of the islands in the lake became a peninsula, exposing the birds to coyotes and other predators. The birds abandoned the island. Some felt the scenic beauty and ecological value of Mono Lake were imperiled, and the Audubon Society sued to enjoin the Water Department from diverting the flow of the streams. They claimed the waters and shores of the lake were protected by public trust. The lower court held for the Water Department.

The California Supreme Court held that the public trust doctrine preserved the sovereign power of the state to protect public trust uses, which included preventing the harm to a public trust like the lake. The Court also held that the human and environmental uses of the lake, uses protected by public trust, deserved to be considered in this action.

Underground Water

There are three legal doctrines for rights to underground water:

- ◆ reasonable use;
- ◆ unlimited use; and,
- ◆ prior use.

Most states have adopted the principle that one must make reasonable use of underground water. Some states have adopted the English rule that one may make unlimited use of such water. And a few western states give greater rights to those who have made previous use of the water.

Notice that the English rule allowing unlimited use of underground water compliments the English rule that water in streams and lakes cannot be interfered with. This is followed in many eastern states where water is plentiful. In California, landowners over a common underground water basin are allowed a proportionate quantity of the water, but may not lower the water table.

Rain

A relatively recent area of dispute between neighbors is when one *steals* the rain from another or causes him to get too much rain. (This is done by *seeding the clouds*.) The general rule in this area is that there is not a right to fly over another person's land to change the weather. Landowners have a right to natural weather without modification. There is a difference, however, where the flight does not go over the landowner's property.

🏠 *A water company was hired by a number of farmers near Fort Stockton, Texas, to participate in a hail suppression program. It would seed the clouds in an attempt to suppress hail. The cloud seeding also destroyed potential rain clouds over the land of several people. They sought and got an injunction that would keep the company from seeding any clouds. The company appealed and the court upheld the injunction as to the lands of those who sued, but stated the injunction was too broad in restraining cloud seeding over the other lands.*

🏠 *When a drought hit Fulton County, Pennsylvania, some of the property owners formed a nonprofit corporation to fight the Blue Ridge Weather Modification Association. that had been trying to stop hail storms in the area. The company had used cloud seeding and 110 ground-based generators of silver iodide to suppress hail in thunder-*

storms passing the area. The first judge assigned to the case died before he could issue an opinion, but the parties waived their right to a new trial. In the meantime, the Pennsylvania legislature passed a law making weather modification illegal in some areas, then repealed the law, and passed another providing that weather modification should be encouraged and licensed. The court ruled that while citizens have a property right in the clouds and moisture, the case was moot since the new law provided for damages to those injured by weather modification.

Artificially Sprayed Water

Water that is sprayed from one property to another is a trespass and can also be a nuisance. Courts can order a stop to such activity.

A luncheonette in the Bronx in New York intended to set up a summer garden in the rear yard of the property it was renting, but water spraying from the property next door made that impossible. The luncheonette sued and was awarded damages for lost value of the property for the sixteen months it could not use the yard.

LIGHT AND AIR

Another area where neighbors have often gotten into disputes is when one person blocks the view, light, or air of another. Such cases have involved fences blocking neighbors' windows, trees blocking their sunlight, and billboards blocking other billboards.

In England, there is a ruling known as the *doctrine of ancient lights*. It holds that people have the right to the light that has reached their property since ancient times. This doctrine forbids people from building structures that block the light. The law started right after the great fire of London in 1666, when much of the city had to be rebuilt.

However, in America, nearly every court has rejected the doctrine of ancient lights. The rationale in this country is that the doctrine is an impediment to technological and industrial progress and that since the advent of electric lights, it is no longer necessary. This position has allowed our country to have some of the largest business districts and highest skyscrapers in the world.

The general rule in America is that people can build structures on their property without regard to the effect on their neighbors' needs or preferences for view, light, or air. (An exception to this is Georgia, where a statute recognizes an easement for light and air.)

> 🏠 *A couple owned an office building on Highway 20 in Fort Dodge, Iowa. A company built a muffler shop, that while complying with the zoning restrictions, blocked the view of the building to traffic approaching from the west on Highway 20. The couple sued the company for unreasonable interference with their lawful use and enjoyment of their property. They also sought abatement of the alleged nuisance. The courts dismissed the suit.*

> 🏠 *In Washington state, a couple owned a nice home on the western slope of Capitol Hill. They bought the home because of the view. They did not think that anything could be built near them. Later, two other couples built two multi-story condominium buildings below them on the hill and blocked their view. They sued, but the court held that blocking a person's view with a building that was otherwise legal was not a nuisance.*

> 🏠 *A six-story building and a four-story building were built side by side in a town in New Hampshire. The six-story building had air conditioners in the fifth and sixth floor windows that hung out over the four-story building. The owner of the four-story building decided to tear it down*

and build a six-story building. This meant that the windows on the fifth and sixth floors of the six story building would be up against a brick wall (and, of course, would not be able to use the air conditioners.) The owner of the six-story building sued and the case went to the New Hampshire Supreme Court. The court held that the owner of the six-story building had no right to stop the neighbor from building directly in front of her windows.

Spite Fences

Though the general rule is that a person has no right to a view over his neighbor's land, there are, of course, exceptions. The main exception regards *spite fences*. This is a fence built by someone solely to harass his neighbor. When a court finds that a fence is merely a spite fence, then the court may order it removed.

Right off the Murdo exit from I-90 in South Dakota, a businessman had maintained a billboard for years and then the neighbor built one blocking it. The South Dakota Supreme Court held that if the placement of the billboard was malicious, it could be ordered to be removed, since it would be a private nuisance. The court held that a property owner has a duty to use his rights thereon in a manner that does not infringe on the rights of another. Maliciously erecting a sign to block the view of another's sign was a nuisance.

Today with billboards falling out of favor and trees gaining more protection, neighbors have had more luck using one against the other.

Example: A person in Florida planted several trees that blocked his neighbor's billboard. The trees were allowed to stay and the billboard became useless.

In some cases, the court may find that a person had both a legitimate and a spiteful purpose for building something and allow it to stay.

🏠 *In Miami, the Fountainebleu Hotel stood north along the beach from the Eden Roc Hotel. The owners did not get along. The owner of the Fountainebleu decided to build an addition that would cast a shadow over the pool and sun deck of the Eden Roc during the middle of the day. The Eden Roc sued to stop construction The Eden Roc lost since the court found that spite was not the sole purpose of building the addition.*

There is one other exception that should be mentioned because it may prove important in the future. It regards solar energy.

🏠 *A couple in Wisconsin had a home heated by solar panels. A neighbor started to build in such a way that the solar panels would be blocked. The case went to the Wisconsin Supreme Court and the Court issued a long opinion explaining that it knew that no court in America recognized the right of access to sunlight, but stated that it thought it was time for a change. It said that since energy conservation was important and would be more so in the future, it was reversing its own past decisions to modernize the law. Therefore, the neighbor was forbidden from blocking the sun from the solar panels.*

It will be many years before we will know if this case is an aberration or a new trend. There are some who argue that the American doctrine is passe and that the law should change. However, other courts considering the issue have not jumped on the bandwagon.

🏠 *In California, a couple built a passive solar house that had large windows facing south to catch the sun. The neighbor, in violation of rules in the area, planted a number of trees that blocked the sun from the couple's windows. The California appellate court decided not to follow Wisconsin's policy. It cited differences such as the fact that in Wisconsin solar panels were blocked, but here it was just a passive solar house. The court also said, as courts often do, that this was an issue for the legislature to change, not the court.*

NOTE: *It is possible that state legislatures will enter the field and declare public policy in this area. In New Mexico, a Solar Rights Act was passed that gives property owners a right to solar energy based upon priority in time.*

As mentioned earlier, one way to obtain the right to view, light, or air is through an easement. If a person owns a large oceanfront lot and sells the half near the water, he or she can put an easement on the oceanfront lot at the time of sale that will forever restrict the use of the lot. For instance, he can put an easement on the property saying that no building may ever be built on the property higher than one story. This way the owner can insure that the second floor view of the ocean will never be blocked.

Lights

Like many areas of neighbor law, lights are usually legal unless they cause a substantial injury and there is no overriding justification. The courts balance the interests of the parties. (However, when baseball or Christmas is involved, the balance may be tilted against the person complaining.)

A racetrack was built across from a drive-in movie theater in Portland, Oregon. The lights for night races made it difficult to see the films. In a lawsuit against the racetrack, the court noted that the movie screen was especially sensitive to light and that it had to be specially recessed from the moon and starlight. It needed other special barriers to make it useful. The court found that the special sensitivity of one neighbor does not make the activity of another neighbor into a nuisance.

🏠 *The owner of a professional baseball club, the Lewiston Indians, leased the baseball field from the local high school for night baseball games. Nearby property owners sued, claiming that their homes were being flooded with excessive light. The games also caused excessive noise and trespass of balls and people onto their properties. Their suit went to the Idaho Supreme Court that held they were entitled to an injunction limiting the lights, hours of the game, and other factors that interfered with their enjoyment of their property.*

🏠 *More than 300 nearby homeowners filed suit against the Louisville Board of Education to stop the installation of lights at the Manual High School stadium for night football. They won their case before the trial court judge, but the school board appealed. The appeals court noted that the nearby homes had increased in value in the last twenty years. It held that in a case like this, the lighting could not be stopped before it was even used. Only if it proved to be an actual nuisance, could it be enjoined.*

🏠 *For several years, a man had maintained an elaborate Christmas display at his residence in Jefferson Parish, Louisiana. Each year the display grew in size and popularity. It included lights and music amplified through loud speakers. After six years, the neighbors claimed it was becoming a nuisance—causing restricted access to their homes, noise, public urination, property damage, and a lack of on-street parking. The local sheriff instituted a traffic control plan using seven deputies and portable toi-*

lets and the parish limited the display to a period of thirty days and only until 11 p.m. in the evening. The neighbors felt that this did not eliminate the problem and filed suit.

In this case, the owner counter-claimed that the restrictions abridged his constitutional rights. The local court refused to stop the display and the neighbors appealed. The appeals court held that the display should not be stopped, but that the regulations were reasonable and not unconstitutional. The neighbors appealed to the Louisiana Supreme Court that held that the display did cause real damage in a residential area and was not just an inconvenience. It entered an injunction against the display.

> *A man opened a root beer stand across from a nice residence in Dallas, Texas. The owner of the residence claimed that in the 20 x 24 foot space of the root beer stand, there were large glaring lights and a red neon sign that reflected into his home. In a lawsuit, he also complained about noise, dust, and obnoxious odors claiming that the stand was a nuisance. The trial court ordered the owner to install lights with colored or shaded globes of a lesser candle power and and to not operate his radio.*

> *The city of High Point, North Carolina constructed a million-gallon, 184-foot-high water tank and painted it a bright silver color. The reflecting sunlight caused a problem for the owners of property on the southeast corner of Salem Street and Bridges Street. The parties sued and won. However, in two separate appeals to the North Carolina Supreme Court, the city won a ruling that limited the owners' rights to compensation.*

Smoke, Dust, and Pollution

Traditionally, the only way to stop pollution was a nuisance suit. If it was a public nuisance, the city could take action. For a private nuisance, affected citizens could go to court. But as we enter the times of greater environmental consciousness, more and more remedies become available.

Besides zoning and land use laws, there are specific pollution laws passed by the state and local governments, as well as the United States Congress. Now, if the local zoning or health official cannot do anything, there are many other state and federal officials whose sole job is to combat pollution. Additionally, many of the anti-pollution laws allow suits by private individuals.

Some of the federal laws that may be useful dealing with a neighborhood pollution situation are:

- *Rivers and Harbors Act of 1899;*
- *Federal Water Pollution Control Act;*
- *National Environmental Policy Act of 1969;*
- *Clean Air Act;*
- *Resource Conservation and Recovery Act of 1976;* and,
- *Comprehensive Environmental Response, Compensation, and Liability Act.*

After the passage of the *National Environmental Policy Act*, many states passed their own environmental policy acts. These acts include such provisions as requiring environmental impact statements and allowing private suits.

Some state constitutions were amended in the 1960s and 1970s to include clauses providing for protection of the environment. Some of these clauses specifically allow for citizen suits to protect the environment and others have been interpreted to do so by the courts.

If there is a neighborhood pollution problem and one of the various government agencies cannot do anything, the nuisance suit is still an available remedy.

🏠 *A dye works was being operated in Chester, Pennsylvania. The neighbors claimed the facility was a nuisance, causing smoke, soot, and fumes. The company brought in witnesses from the neighborhood who testified that they hung waitress uniforms and chiropodist towels out to dry and they were not affected by any smoke or soot. This convinced the court that it was not bad enough to be a nuisance.*

🏠 *When the garbage dump in the city of Ann Arbor, Michigan, became objectionable and nearly full, the city began looking for another site. After three and a half years, it found a parcel about a mile north of the city with a ravine suitable for dumping. The city began using the ravine as a dump. Neighbors in the area filed suit against the city to stop the use of the land as a dump. The trial court ruled for the neighbors, enjoining use of the land as a dump, and the city appealed.*

In this case, the Supreme Court of Michigan reversed the decision and allowed the dump to continue. It noted that there was nowhere in the city for a dump and the surrounding county had made it illegal to start a new dump, however the court ordered the city to eliminate the most objectionable features of the dump.

🏠 *The state health commissioner decided to crack down on the garbage dumps in Montgomery County, Ohio. Nine suits were filed; one of them against the operators of the South Dayton Dump. The Supreme Court of Ohio noted that both dumping and burning of garbage had been a problem in the state for many years and that it was clearly a nuisance. The court gave the owners of the dumps just thirty days to complete their burning operations. The*

company then had to convert to a sanitary landfill opera-
tion where the garbage would be buried each day.

Odors

Obnoxious odors have often been held to be a nuisance. The factors
to be considered in deciding whether a smell is obnoxious are:
whether the smells are unusual for the location and whether they
would offend someone of ordinary sensibilities. For instance, fish
hanging in the sun to dry might be normal in a seaside market, but
if a fisherman took them home to a residential neighborhood and
hung them in his yard every day, it would probably be considered a
nuisance.

🏠 *A woman operated a kennel about a mile outside of*
Grand Rapids, Michigan. It was in an area with several
commercial establishments and about a quarter mile from
about twenty homes. Several neighbors brought a suit
against the owner claiming that the kennel was a nui-
sance to the area because of the smells and noise. They
provided evidence that it was a nuisance and she pro-
vided evidence that it was not. The judge visited the
kennel and found the testimony about the problems was
exaggerated. He also noted that the owner installed a gas
incinerator that remedied the problem with the odors and
ruled that he would not order to stop operating the kennel.
A neighbor appealed to the Supreme Court of Michigan
that ruled that no one is entitled to air utterly uncontami-
nated by any odor whatsoever.

🏠 *In Wilmington, Delaware, the residents of Westhaven*
Development brought an action against a neighbor to
enjoin him from storing 360 tons of horse manure on the
land next to their homes. They claimed the manure gave
off an extremely offensive stench; contaminated the air of

*the neighborhood; that flies germinated in large numbers
and swarmed around Westhaven homes; and as a result,
many families had been made uncomfortable and sick,
and living in Westhaven had become unbearable. (The
manure was stored outside during the spring and summer
for use in his mushroom houses.)*

In this case, the court held that the manure had substantially impaired reasonable comfort and could constitute a nuisance. The fact that his mushroom houses and manure storage had been going on for twelve years before Westhaven was built, would not keep the residents from obtaining injunctive relief. The residents had met the burden of establishing their case by clear and convincing proof. The court granted the injunction.

🏠 *A farmer was feeding 600 hogs on his farm with garbage
obtained from the city of Dayton. The garbage was in various stages of decay and produced noxious odors. Many
complaints were lodged concerning the odors. A health
officer investigated and found the condition created a
nuisance and ordered the farmer to abate the nuisance.
He did not obey the order and the health commissioner
brought suit. The court held that the system of garbage
distribution employed by the farmer should be discontin-
ued. The practice was unsanitary and posed potential
health risks. The feeding of garbage to the hogs constituted a nuisance and ordered it stopped.*

ELECTRONIC WAVES

Radio, television, telephone, and other electromagnetic waves are a relatively new topic for the legal system. However, principles used in related areas have been used when problems with these matters have come up.

Generally, like the situation with view, light, and air, courts have found no rights to the reception of electromagnetic waves. An owner of property can build upon his property without worry about the effect on TV or radio reception at neighboring properties.

🏠 When Sears Roebuck & Co. began building their 110-story headquarters in Chicago, surrounding property owners were concerned that it would disturb their radio and television reception. The Illinois Supreme Court ruled that unless there was a law against it, a landowner had a right to construct a 110-story building. Television reception was not a right protected by law.

If a person produces electromagnetic waves and these cause a problem for the neighbors, this is a completely different situation and the waves produced can be deemed a nuisance.

🏠 An appliance store in Shenandoah, Iowa noticed that the reception of its televisions had suddenly deteriorated after a new computer system was installed at a nearby travel agency. The computer company technicians made several service calls to investigate the problem, but it turned out to be a design problem and not a service problem. The appliance store was told that computer company was "way over budget" on the computer and "if you don't like it you can move." The appliance store filed suit and won. The court rejected the argument that the televisions were an extra sensitive use of the property that would have precluded a finding of nuisance.

If the party having the problems with the electricity does not do everything in his or her power to alleviate the problem, then damages may not be allowed for collection.

🏠 After a couple had an electrical system installed on their dairy farm in Wisconsin, they started having problems with their cows. Many cows exhibited violent or erratic behavior. The herd suffered excessive and chronic masti-

tis. Their milk production declined and many cows had to be culled. In a lawsuit against the supplier that was appealed both to the Court of Appeals and the Wisconsin Supreme Court, the couple was awarded $300,000 in damages. It was later reduced to $200,000 because the jury believed the couple was one-third at fault.

When the power lines are legally constructed not much can be done about them.

🏠 *When Central Power Company began distributing electric power in Bucyrus, Ohio, the residents along Southern Avenue were upset that a 66,000 volt line was to run down their street. They filed suit, but the court held that high voltage lines are not a nuisance unless they are not constructed properly. Putting a pole in the middle of someone's driveway was actionable, however, and the owners whose driveways were blocked were entitled to injunctions.*

However, federal law has pre-empted state law in many areas, such as for radio and television broadcasts.

🏠 *When a couple experienced radio and television interference and other disruptions that they believed were caused by their neighbor, they filed suit in state court for nuisance. The court found that only the FCC had jurisdiction dismissed the case. They appealed to the Arizona Court of Appeals that held the same. The couple then appealed to the United States District Court in Arizona that also said that electromagnetic interference by radio transmitters were under the exclusive jurisdiction of the FCC and dismissed the case. (Presumably the FCC had previously elected not to take any action.)*

RADIOACTIVITY

Leakage of radiation from a nearby facility can be one of the most frightening events in a homeowner's life. Besides the devastation to property values, there is the risk of cancer and future birth defects.

The law regarding radioactivity is, in most respects, controlled by the *Atomic Energy Act of 1954*. While state law determines general principles of liability, many of the ultimate issues are determined by federal law and regulation.

There have been several instances of neighbors of nuclear facilities attempting court action. Many of the legal issues have been settled. The courts have ruled that the federal government has the exclusive power to regulate radiological hazards. However, the states are allowed to regulate hazards caused by a nuclear facility that are not of a radiological nature. This means a state court could declare a facility a nuisance for any reason other than one based upon a radiological hazard.

> 🏠 *A resident of Midland County, Michigan, sued to stop the construction of a pressurized water nuclear power plant on the Tittabawassee River. Since the plant was only one mile from his home, he claimed the nuclear power plant would be a private and public nuisance jeopardizing his health, depreciating his property value, and interfering with the use and enjoyment of his property. The lower court held for the power company. The Court of Appeals held that state courts could not consider the allegations dealing with the possibility of nuclear accident, as that was the federal government's domain. State courts however, could consider the allegations of non-radiological hazards from the plant. If a state court did find a nuisance to exist, it could require the plant to abate the nuisance, but could not prohibit construction of the plant. The court held that the resident had failed to show a present or definite future nuisance and affirmed the lower holding.*

🏠 *The New Jersey Department of Environmental Protection sought and won a judgment holding a nuclear power plant responsible when a large number of fish were killed by a discharge of cold water. However, this was reversed by the New Jersey Supreme Court that held such a judgment would infringe on the subject of radiological hazards. It noted that the shutdown was required by rules of the Atomic Energy Commission because of a coolant leak.*

🏠 *A limited partnership with a general partner based in Texas, decided that Colorado was a good place to invest. The partnership bought some land in Jefferson County, Colorado, near the Rocky Flats Nuclear Plant. As it turned out, the investment was a poor one as the land was contaminated by plutonium, americium, and uranium and was unfit for either residential or commercial development. After over six years of litigation, the Federal District Court in Colorado held that since there was no showing of violation of any Environmental Protection Agency standards, the issues were pre-empted by federal law. The issues involved were largely political and it had no power to take action. The court noted that the owners of the land could show nothing more than potential harm from the radioactive chemicals on their property and that this was not a trespass.*

In this case, it was appealed to the United States Court of Appeals for the Tenth Circuit that reversed the ruling. The court held that this case was similar to the Karen Silkwood case and that state law was not pre-empted by the *Atomic Energy Act* in cases like this involving negligence, trespass, and nuisance. It noted that in cases like this, there was no administrative remedy available.

–6–
AVOIDING A
NEIGHBOR DISPUTE

You may not realize it, but the last thing you need is a long, drawn-out neighbor dispute. It takes up too much of your time and money and puts you through unnecessary stress. Here are some actions to take in order to avoid a lengthy neighbor dispute.

TALK IT OVER

Believe it or not, some neighbors would be glad to stop annoying you. They might not even know that what they're doing is annoying you. So before you take any drastic action against your neighbor, try to approach them about it.

Unlike the 1950s, when most wives stayed home and were friends with other wives in the neighborhood, today many of us do not even know our neighbors. With both spouses working and many other obligations to attend to, for some of us the closest contact we have with our neighbors is to wave as we drive away. Many of us do not even know our neighbors' names.

It is easy to get angry with and build up resentment toward someone we don't know. If the only thing we know about them is that they play the piano at 11 p.m. on nights that we have to get to sleep early, it is easy to build up resentment.

However, they may be oblivious to the fact that we can hear it and need to get up. Maybe they're just having a good time and assuming that if anyone was annoyed, he or she would complain.

Some people would be mortified to know that they were causing any offense in the neighborhood and would be ever so glad to rectify it. So the first thing you should do is explain the situation to them.

Of course, do not be confrontational about it. If there is time, you should try to meet them first and talk about some friendly matter. Compliment their children or do something else to make them feel good. Then, when they trust you as a friend, *mention* the problem. If you can think of a simple solution, suggest it. If Monday mornings you have to get up extra early to fly out of town, explain that any night, except Sunday night, would not be a problem for the piano playing.

Tenants

If the problem is caused by an individual who doesn't own the property, but is a tenant, you might get some help from the landlord. While he won't want to lose a paying tenant, the property is an investment and he sure won't want it to go down in value. Point out that the tenant's actions could be lowering the property values in the neighborhood and are likely to cause similar problems at neighboring properties.

ABATEMENT

One way to solve a nuisance is to take care of it yourself. Of course this does not work for all problems, but many can be solved this way. If your neighbor's tree roots are invading your property, you can cut them off at the property line or if a branch of his tree is rubbing against your roof, you can trim it. You can even go onto your neighbor's property to abate a nuisance if it can be done peacefully and without causing harm to his property. If his pump is making too much noise, you may be able to put oil on it. If his sprinkler is spraying onto your porch, you can turn it away. Use your judgment. Occasionally a person abating a nuisance gets sued for trespassing, but in many cases it can be done peacefully.

As with most legal rights, the right to *abate* a nuisance requires reasonableness. The person must act at a reasonable time of day and in a reasonable manner. What is reasonable depends upon the circumstances at the time. In an emergency, it would be more reasonable to take drastic measures than if there were no emergency. A person causing damage to another's property while abating a nuisance can be held liable for the damage.

🏠 *In Rhode Island in the 1890s, a property owner put a gate across a road blocking the access to the beach. Another man needed to go to the beach to get seaweed that he had a legal right to do. So he got a friend to come with him and together they tried to crash the gate with an ox cart. An altercation ensued with the owner who was injured. The two who tried to crash the gate were arrested for "assault with intent to kill and murder" and were found guilty. The court said that even if the owner was creating a public nuisance by blocking the road, the others did not have the right to stop him with violence.*

AVOIDANCE

Sometimes, the best way to solve a problem with a neighbor is to avoid it. Depending upon the nature of the problem, you can stay out of the neighbor's path, park somewhere else, buy earplugs, or, move from the neighborhood entirely. This is often the best solution as far as your nerves and your wallet are concerned.

–7–
WINNING A
NEIGHBOR DISPUTE

If a dispute with your neighbor is inevitable, you at least want to be sure you can win. To do so, research your problem to be sure you are legally in the right. Next, review the methods in this chapter to find the best one that suits your dispute.

NEIGHBORHOOD ASSOCIATION

If you live in a *condominium, mobile home park, planned unit development,* or other community with rules and regulations, you may be able to get the governing body to take action. Most likely this won't cost you anything. Check the rules governing your community and see if there is something covering the specific problem. Be sure to get the most recent and complete set of rules. Sometimes these are amended over the years.

If the neighbor's behavior is against any of the rules, you can file a complaint with the board that is in charge of enforcement. If you find other neighbors who are bothered by the activity, this can also help.

If there is no board in charge of such matters, for example in a residential subdivision merely subject to deed restrictions, you may need to file a lawsuit. A letter from a lawyer pointing out the violation is often enough to gain compliance.

GOVERNMENTAL INTERVENTION

If you do not live in a community with regulations, there may be a law or governmental regulation that will solve your problem. You may have noticed in recent years the proliferation of laws in this country covering many aspects of our lives. In some areas of the country, it is illegal to water plants at certain hours; park vehicles in front of one's house; cut down trees on one's own property; or, use a clothesline in one's yard. If your neighbor is doing something bothersome to you, check to see if there is a governmental regulation.

There are a number of governmental agencies that may be able to help with your problem. Call every department that sounds like it covers your problem. Once you find one that does, don't stop there. Call a few more. Maybe you can get two or three agencies to work with you. When dealing with governmental agencies, remember that you are not dealing with a private enterprise. Most are still typical bureaucracies, and as such, it takes considerable effort to get action.

In some cases, government functionaries are not fully aware of their own rules or what they mean. If a government agent says he or she cannot help you, ask if any other person or agency can, and if not, do some research yourself.

In most cases, you have a right to copies of all government codes and regulations. Some government entities will have them on the Internet, but others may only have them in the libraries or government offices.

One thing to keep in mind is that not all government regulations or laws are enforceable. Just because a majority of a government board wants to forbid something, doesn't mean they can. The state and federal constitutions both limit government action and laws and regulations are often thrown out by judges.

If you are the one being pursued by a neighbor for a purported violation, you should make sure any law or regulation is valid. If your rights to use your property are being limited by a law or regulation, consider whether this limitation violates any of your constitutional rights. (See the section in Chapter 1 for information about constitutional rights.) You may want to get a lawyer's opinion on whether a law or regulation is valid.

Criminal Laws

In some cases the actions of your neighbor may be against a criminal law, not just a local regulation. In such cases, enforcement may be much easier. The government will go to court for you and the offender will have considerable expense defending himself. A neighbor faced with criminal charges may find it easier to stop being a nuisance than to fight the government.

THIRD-PARTY INTERVENTION

If you can't solve the problem yourself and there is no clear rule or law being violated, the next thing you should try is *mediation* or *arbitration*. Some people think these two ways of solving a disagreement are the same—but they are very different.

Mediation

When people present their dispute to a person who helps them come to a resolution it is called *mediation*. The mediator is usually trained in psychology and dispute resolution. The function of the mediator is to help the parties understand each other's side and to guide them to a mutually agreeable resolution. Perhaps he or she will ask each side to argue the other's side's case. The idea is to get both sides to see the big picture and find a solution both are happy with. This ends in a win-win situation.

Arbitration

Arbitration is similar to a lawsuit. An arbitrator takes the place of the judge. The parties ask the arbitrator to make a decision for them. If the parties agree ahead of time to be bound by the decision of the arbitrator, whatever it is, this is called *binding arbitration*. This means that the parties have agreed that they have no right to appeal the decision of the arbitrator. The advantage of arbitration over a lawsuit is that it is faster and less expensive. Lawsuits involve elaborate rules covering court procedure and evidence. They must be fit into the schedules of the overcrowded courts.

Deciding on the Best Method for Resolution

The decision of whether one or the other should be used in lieu of a lawsuit should be based upon the facts of the case and how much you wish to spend on it. As can be seen from some of the sample cases in this book, many people spent a lot of money over disputes that were only worth a few dollars. But for them, the principle was important.

If you feel that most anyone would agree that your neighbor is being unreasonable, then mediation or arbitration may be better. You might be able to get an unbiased opinion of your case from an attorney who offers a *free initial consultation* on your matter. An attorney who handles arbitration, as well as trials, would usually be better than one who only does trials.

If you weren't able to solve your neighbor dispute with the methods in Chapter 6 and you haven't been able to win it as explained in this chapter, then your next step would be to go to court as discussed in Chapter 9.

—8—
PROBLEMS WITH GOVERNMENT AGENCIES

When it comes to problems with government agencies, you usually have two choices: make the fight the center of your life or stay under the radar screen. Governments have nearly unlimited resources. Even a small town government can get the money it needs to fight you by raising taxes (including the taxes you pay). Also, the arbiter of a dispute with the government is always a government official, be it a local committee or a federal judge. So the cards are stacked against you from the start. But the situation is not hopeless. There are judges who will support the individual.

The two most important things to consider when beginning to fight the government is whether in fact you are right and whether you have the time and money it will take to prove you are right. If you are clearly in the right and the government is abusing its powers, you can do a service to your fellow citizens by fighting for your own rights.

Local government boards are often made up of fellow citizens with little knowledge of the law. Oftentimes they have strong prejudices and a desire to have things go their way regardless of others' rights. Unless the agency has an attorney well versed in constitutional law, it can easily get carried away in ruling a community. By knowing what your rights are you can be sure that they don't do anything outside of their legitimate powers.

The rule of reasonableness controls most aspects of neighbor law. While a judge will usually try to do what is fair, this does not always apply to the government. Government policies do not always have to be fair. The government has wide power to achieve its goals and those goals are usually what a majority of the elected officials say they are. Only when government goals violate rights guaranteed in the state or federal constitutions are they limited or struck down.

When it comes to problems with agencies of the government, the most important rights you have are the federal constitutional rights as explained in Chapter 1. If a government action does not violate a constitutional right, it is probably enforceable, even if it does not seem fair. This is because government actions are usually *presumed* to be valid.

If your dispute does not come under any federal constitutional right, check your *state constitution.* You may be surprised at some of the rights you have.

> **Example:** In Delaware, the state constitution states:
> *A person has the right to keep and bear arms for the defense of self, family, home and State, and for hunting and recreational use.*

If a local ordinance forbids someone in Delaware from possessing a gun, the state constitution would offer him some relief.

If a government action does not violate a constitutional right it may be invalid if it does not comply with state law.

> **Example:** In Florida, the cities often try to hold homeowners liable for water bills that their tenants build up. However, state law forbids cities from doing this. Until someone points this law out to the city officials, many of them keep trying to bill the homeowners and refuse to provide them with water.

Lastly, if some local governmental rule seems unfair, then you might want to get it changed. Most elected officials and successful *referendums* are voted for by only a small number of the citizens. This is because in many elections only about half the qualified people vote. If you feel that a law should be changed and think that most people would agree with you, you can probably get it done if you put out the effort.

EMINENT DOMAIN

Eminent domain is when the government takes property from a private citizen for a public purpose. For instance, when a new expressway is built, the government will condemn all the properties in its path and buy them from the owners. There are no exact figures on how much property is taken by the government for private purposes. According to the *Institute for Justice*, a public interest law firm, there were over 10,000 filed or threatened takings of property for private use written about in newspapers between 1998 and 2002. In the one state where the exact figures are known, there were 17 times as many as reported in the newspapers. So the actual number throughout the country is huge.

Fair Compensation

It is clear that under the Fifth Amendment to the United States Constitution, the government must pay for property it takes from its citizens. A big issue in eminent domain cases is *fair compensation*. In some instances, the owners might get a very generous payment, but in others, the payment might be below *fair market value*.

In some states, besides being paid for their property, the owners will have their attorney's fees and appraisal fees paid by the government. In other states, they must pay for these things themselves. An example of a property owner getting a good deal from eminent domain is if the state takes a few feet of property to widen a road. In such a situation, the owner might not need that particular piece of land, but could be paid a per-square-foot price based on the value of his whole property.

An example of a property owner getting a bad deal from eminent domain is that a family has lived on a property for several generations and loses all of it at *below* market value. Even fair market value couldn't repay a family in such a situation. The family would never find a property with equal value to them.

Private Purpose vs. Public Purpose

Another big issue, besides price in eminent domain cases, is whether the purpose for which property is being taken is actually a public purpose. Some states allow property to be taken from one private owner and sold to another private owner, for example, to build a shopping mall. In such cases, the government argues that since the mall will help the community, the purpose is public. But the actual owners of the mall are private and they are the ones making a profit from the land being taken from other property owners.

From the 1700s until 1954, property could only be taken for clearly public purpose. But in that year, the United States Supreme Court approved the taking of slum property to be used by private parties for urban renewal. At first only blighted properties were taken. But in recent years, governments have taken properties that were perfectly fine on the reasoning that the newly planned use for the property was good for the entire community.

In some states, owners can refuse to sell and delay the process for years. In others the government is allowed to deposit the estimated value of the property with the court and immediately evict the owner and tear the property down. Even if the owner eventually wins, the family home is already demolished.

If you receive notice that the government wants to take your property check with a lawyer and see what your rights are under your state's laws. Also, check with the *Institute for Justice* as it sometimes provides lawyers for these types of cases. You can contact the institute at their web site at:

www.ij.org

Another group, the *Castle Coalition*, has an *Eminent Domain Abuse Survivors Guide* and a web site explaining, in detail, how to fight the condemnation of your property. Find both of these sources of assistance on their web site at:

www.CastleCoalition.org

AIRCRAFT AND AIRPORTS

The original concept of *property ownership* included the notion that ownership of land included the space from the center of the earth up into endless space. A famous statement by Lord Coke, *"cujus est solum ejus est usque ad coelum"* (he who owns the soil owns upward to heaven), was quoted often in the days before the invention of the airplane.

However, new technology has required a change in the principles of law. If flying over private property were to be considered trespass today, then the airlines would all be out of business. This fast change in the notion of property rights in response to the invention of flight is a good example of how flexible our system of law is—and must be.

In the United States, the right of airplanes to fly over private property is controlled by federal laws and regulations. The laws are contained in the United States Code, Title 49. This law gives any U.S. citizen a "right of freedom of transit through the navigable air space of the United States." The navigable air space is defined to include different altitudes depending upon the location. Airplanes flying at these levels cannot be guilty of trespass.

Even though flying over a person's property is not trespass, the noise, vibrations, and dangers associated with airplane flights and airports can be a nuisance. If any of these factors are bothersome to a large part of the community, then it may be considered a public nuisance and may be stopped by government action. If only one or a few property owners are bothered, then it *may* be a private nuisance.

> **Example:** When a man obtained a permit to build an airport in New Jersey, his neighbors filed suit to stop the construction. The court ruled that since an airport was a lawful business, it would not stop the construction. However, if the airport became a nuisance, the neighbors may file for compensation.

🏠 *A man owned a 135-acre estate in Richmond Heights, Ohio for twenty-five years, when a company purchased land next door for an airport and flying school. The company built a hanger for twenty planes and planned three more. They also planned parking for 460 automobiles. The neighbor filed suit in federal court. The court did an analysis of the law of rights to the sky from the year 1200 to the present. The court noted that aviation was a growing field that was encouraged by the government and that it had contributed millions of dollars to the economy of Ohio. It concluded that the airport was not necessarily a nuisance, but that certain activities, such as creating too much dust or flying lower than 500 feet could be stopped.*

If a court decides that the flights of airplanes are a legal nuisance, then there are two primary remedies. The court can order the flights to be stopped, limited, or it can order payment to the injured neighbor for the damages suffered due to the flights.

🏠 *A man in Macomb County, Michigan, started using part of his land for an airstrip. His neighbor complained that the planes scared his cattle and that the noise was a nuisance. When he expanded the use of the airstrip, began giving flying lessons, and started allowing others to use the airstrip, the neighbor filed suit. The court ruled that the flights had become a nuisance and it ordered the man to only use the airstrip for his personal use. Years later when the neighbor died and the airport owner obtained state and federal approval for expanded use of his airstrip, the court refused to dissolve the injunction because it would still constitute a nuisance to the man's widow.*

🏠 *Neighboring property owners brought suit against the Valley Forge Airport located near the village of Audubon in Pennsylvania. They claimed the airplanes made such loud noises as to disturb their sleep, conversations, and general enjoyment of their property. The court held that this airport was in a rural area and was operated reasonably except for night flying. It balanced the property owners' rights against the nation's need for expanding the then-experimental stages of aviation. The court refused to stop the flights completely, but enjoined the airport from operating after 10 p.m.*

Where monetary damages are awarded, these may be for actual losses to the neighbor, such as broken windows or they may be compensation for the diminished value of the property.

Example 1: The Keene, New Hampshire airport took part of a neighboring woman's land through *eminent domain* in order to expand. Later, it used the property near her home for a jet warm-up area. This caused noise and dust and broken windows in her home. She was awarded damages.

Example 2: A man in Rye, New Hampshire refused to cooperate in his neighbor's efforts to build an airport on the neighbor's property. The neighbor wanted him to sell or clear his land. When the man failed to do so, the neighbor went onto his land and cut down trees and cleared the land himself. A jury later awarded damages to the property owner for the trees and for the diminished value of his land due to the plane *flyovers*.

If a person is awarded damages for the diminished value of his property because of flights at a neighboring airport, then future owners of that piece of property cannot claim damages. The theory is that when the first owner is paid for the diminished value of his property, he can now sell it for that much less and come out even. Sometimes future owners do not pay less for the property and expect to be paid by the airport again.

Some courts have not been sympathetic to neighbors who live near airports. It may be because of the perceived value of air travel or the fact that the people knew there was an airport nearby when they bought their property, but the neighbors don't always win their suits.

🏠 *When the city of Atlanta constructed a new runway at their airport, it ended about 500 yards from the property of the neighboring landowner. The planes on the runway continually flew just 50 to 100 feet directly over the owner's home. When he brought a suit, it was dismissed; but when he appealed, the court ruled that while the federal government has the right to regulate airspace, it does not have the right to invade property rights. It concluded that he did have a claim against the airport.*

🏠 *When the Atlanta airport expanded again in the 1990s, it developed a plan to buy and tear down single-family houses in the area, but not multifamily rentals, reasoning that "people who own and reside in single-family residences...are more sensitive to aircraft noise levels than those who live in apartments or other rental multifamily residences." Apparently the renters didn't feel that way, for after the area was made a wasteland, the occupancy rates and rental rates of the rentals both went down. The owners of the multifamily buildings sued and the court ruled that there was no rational basis to make such a distinction and that the decision violated the constitution.*

🏠 *The federal government decided to conduct sonic boom tests over Oklahoma City to find out if they would upset the public or damage buildings. Some of the residents of Oklahoma City did get upset and filed suit in federal district court to stop the flights. In ruling against the people, the court said that the citizens did not establish any actual damages and that if they did, they could sue for a monetary award. Therefore, there was no need to stop the flights.*

🏠 *Property owners around General Mitchell Field near Milwaukee, Wisconsin filed suit in federal court against the airport and several airlines claiming that the flights were a nuisance, a violation of federal rules and regulations, and a taking of their property. The court held that the property owners must first complain to the FAA about the violation of federal regulation. If the airport did comply, there could be no nuisance since the federal rules preempt nuisance law. It held that the taking claim could not be made against the airlines, only the airport. It noted that an inverse condemnation claim had already been filed in a state court and that it would retain jurisdiction until the state court action is decided.*

Where the flights are made by agents of the United States government and actual harm is caused to private parties, the United States Supreme Court has recognized a type of remedy other than nuisance. This is based upon the Fifth Amendment to the United States Constitution that states that no property may be taken from citizens without just compensation. The theory is that when a government action causes a person a financial loss, that action is a *taking* of property and must be compensated.

The United States was conducting low altitude flights over the land of a farmer. These flights frightened his chickens, lowering their production, forcing him to go out of business. The United States Supreme Court ruled that this amounted to a taking of his property and that under the constitution he must be compensated.

🏠 *A couple lived 1500 feet from the end of a runway at Portland International Airport. Their home was directly under some flight paths and near others. Because of the noise from the jets using the runways, their property was unusable. They sued and the court ruled that since the flights were more than 500 feet over their property and sometimes not directly over their property, they were not entitled to compensation. They were not happy with this ruling and appealed to the Oregon Supreme Court.*

In this case, the court ruled that noise could be serious enough to amount to a taking of their property, even if the flights were not directly over their property.

🏠 *Around the same time, some people had a similar problem in Kansas. When Topeka Army Air Field was deactivated after World War II some nearby land was platted into a residential subdivision and homes were built in it and sold. A few years later, the base was reopened as Forbes Air Force Base and expanded for the use of jet planes. Although the planes usually did not fly over the homes in the subdivision, their flights caused windows and dishes to rattle, smoke to blow into the homes, and noise that interfered with the residents' enjoyment of their homes. They sued the United States government saying that the value of their homes had been taken by the government and should be compensated. (Federal courts are less sympathetic to people who are harmed by flights that are not directly over their property.) The federal courts ruled against them.*

🏠 *Several residents near the Burbank-Glendale-Pasadena Airport brought a suit against it for inverse condemnation for monetary damages for the lost value of their property. Their suit was dismissed, but the Supreme Court of California said that they could sue the airport. It noted that they could not interfere with the commercial flight patterns and schedules, but that they could sue for inverse condemnation. The airport appealed to the U. S. Supreme Court, but the Court refused to hear the case.*

🏠 *Los Angeles International Airport is one of the largest commercial aviation facility in America. In the late 1960's, the nearby residents found that the noise from the jets on the north runways was so loud that they could not conduct normal conversations, hear their televisions, talk on the phone, and that their children could not study. When they sued, forty-one of them were awarded a total of $86,000 in damages, but the airport did not have to pay their $200,000 attorney's fee, because they sued under a nuisance theory, not an inverse condemnation theory.*

One solution used by some neighbors of airports is to build tall structures on their property that prohibit low-altitude, take-offs and landings. This can force the airport owner to point the runways in another direction. However, some courts have ruled that if there is no legitimate purpose for the structure and it is just to harass the airport owner, *it may be a nuisance.*

🏠 *A man had operated a small private airport in Panama City for four years when another man bought the land north of the airport with the intention of opening a drive-in theater. The airport owner sought to stop the owner from doing this on the grounds the theater would constitute a nuisance and hazard to the planes. The trial court held for the theater owner. The Florida Supreme Court affirmed, holding that the airport owner had not shown that the theater would add measurably to the already existing hazards of lights, poles, and electrical wires. He also had not shown that traffic problems created by the entering and exiting of the theater patrons would constitute a public nuisance.*

🏠 *A man owned a farm next to a small airport. He placed six, thirty-foot poles on his land in line with the runway. The airport paid him a specific amount of money to remove them for a year, and he did. However, he then notified the airport that unless they paid him for another year, he would replace the poles. He sought an injunction from low-flying planes. He claimed he was trying to protect his farm and family and that he wanted an injunction from anything that violated his rights in living in his home and cultivating his field. The court noted that due to the changing direction of winds, the planes sometimes had to take off and land over his land. In doing so, they could fly as low as twenty or thirty feet over the fence that is the common dividing line between the two properties.*

In this case, the farmer's son's testimony indicated that the flying of planes had not interfered with the use of the land for farming purposes. The court decided the farmer was trying to extort money by erecting the poles. And based upon the facts that the airport was operated only in the daytime and operated in a reasonable manner—the court denied his requests.

Large airports cannot be built without careful scrutiny of zoning laws and proper permits, but in some cases zoning laws may be useful in abating a nuisance caused by private aircraft.

🏠 *When the inventor of the Segway built a helipad on his property in Bedford, New Hampshire, so that he could commute to work by helicopter, none of his neighbors objected, except for one. The zoning board granted his permit to build the helipad, saying that nothing in the zoning ordinance prohibited it. The local court threw out the neighbor's suit, noting that there were no laws against helipads. The neighbor then appealed to the Supreme Court of New Hampshire. The Court ruled that since the zoning ordinance was worded to permit no uses other than those specified, and that since helipad uses were not specified in the law, such use was improper. He also held that the use of a helipad could not be accepted as a normal accessory use to a residence without a specific finding and ruling on that point.*

HISTORICAL BUILDINGS

Because historical buildings add character to a neighborhood, residents of the neighborhood often put great value in preserving the most important structures. Where people join together to purchase the structures, there is usually no problem. They can do what they wish with what they own. Problems come up when people attempt to control property owned by others. This is especially true when the owner has other, more profitable plans for the property.

Where a local government designates an area as an historic district, it has been held that owners can be kept from altering, demolishing, or building new structures in the area. This is done under the rationale that historic districts "promote the general welfare" and that is a valid use of government power.

🏠 *In order to preserve the character of its historic district, the City of Santa Fe, New Mexico, passed a law in 1957 requiring buildings to conform with the Old Santa Fe Style, including a rule controlling the size of windows. In order to conform to the size requirements, building owners were required to use wooden dividers to make large panes appear small. After completion of their building, a company removed the window dividers. The company was convicted of the crime of violating the building code. They appealed to the Supreme Court of New Mexico that held that the city had the power to require buildings to conform to their list of historical standards. The court also held that the fact that other buildings in the area had windows that violated the rules was no defense.*

🏠 *In New Orleans, the city government designated a certain area as an historic district and made it illegal to do any construction. A man wanted to build an apartment complex in place of a Victorian cottage and was refused permission. He went to federal court over the issue and the court held that such a law was a valid exercise of government power. He argued that the law constituted a taking of his property and that he should be compensated. This argument was rejected by the court.*

When a city designates one building as a landmark, rather than a whole area, and forbids any alteration to it, the issue is not so clear that there has not been a taking of the owner's property that should be compensated.

🏠 *The landmark case in the area of historical buildings concerns the Penn Central terminal in New York City. In that case, the owners wanted to build a huge office building on the site, but were prevented by the city that designated the building as a landmark. The owners went to court. New York's highest court ruled that the city's action was valid. It noted numerous factors as justification, such as: the owners could make a reasonable return on the property if they operated it efficiently; the claim that society gave value to the property; and, the city gave the owners transferable development rights that could be used elsewhere in the city or could be sold to other prop-*

erty owners. The owners appealed their case to the United States Supreme Court and the New York decision was affirmed.

Since that case was decided, courts have begun to give more weight to the rights of property owners. Today this case might be decided differently. But because of this Supreme Court decision, judges wanting to rule for the owner must find other factors in a case to differentiate it.

BUILDING DEPARTMENTS

One of the most common contact a homeowner has with a government agency is with the building department. While some areas still allow an owner much freedom to remodel his home as he wishes, other require permits and inspections of every little change from changing a light switch to replacing an old fence.

As explained elsewhere, building codes in most areas are so strict that nearly every property can be found to have violations. So anyone giving trouble to the building department can easily be made to pay thousands of dollars for repairs and upgrades. While you can make a good argument that this violates equal protection and discrimination laws, those would be expensive arguments to make.

For this reason, the best way to deal with building departments is to become their friend and let them know you want to do everything right. Before you undertake a major project, stop by the building department, ask to meet the inspector, and explain that you want to be sure to do everything right. Ask for all the rules and for tips of how you should proceed.

While some personnel won't want to be bothered and will tell you to hire someone or look it up yourself, others will be more than happy to share their expertise. Let them know how grateful you are and how much you respect their superior knowledge. If they point out something you've done wrong, tell them how sorry you are, and ask for their opinion on the best way to fix it. When an inspector visits your project, try to become friends. Ask questions on how you can make the project run smoother and make his inspection job easier.

If you just can't get along with an inspector, you may want to go up the chain of command and talk either to his boss or a higher level of city government. Rather than fight the existing rules, go with the attitude that you want to obey the rules, but this inspector is making it too difficult or is not treating all people equally. (Remember that many people in government love the power of their positions and being respectful of their power is usually more successful than fighting their power.)

If they are absolutely violating your rights and it is worth your time and money to wage a battle with them—go to court. If it is clear that a government official is not following the law, you may be able to get a judge to order them to follow the law. This is usually in a court action called *mandamus*. However, a court action for mandamus is usually a very complicated one and unless you have done a lot of legal research, you will need to hire a lawyer.

If you can find a lawyer who will give you an initial consultation for free, you can find out if you have a case worth fighting. Often it is good to get a couple opinions. Always seek-out an attorney with experience with your exact type of case. While all lawyers can practice all types of cases, only the ones with experience in a specific area can give you a good answer without a lot of legal research.

Ignoring Permit Requirements

Working on one's home without getting a permit may be as common a violation as jaywalking in America. Nearly every homeowner has done something, from installing a new ceiling fan to adding an addition on the house, without getting the proper permit and inspections. However, doing so is not without risk. You should know and weigh those risks *before* you proceed.

The first risk is that if you do something wrong, you or a member of your family could be injured or killed. If you are not knowledgeable about electrical systems or ceiling structures, you should not undertake such projects without professional guidance.

The money you save installing a new electrical device in the bathroom will not be worth the risk of electrocution if you do it wrong.

If you do know how to handle home repairs, then the risk of doing them without a permit will be whatever penalties are imposed by your municipality. In some areas, you are merely required to pay for a permit after you are caught, sometimes with a penalty. In other areas, you can be forced to tear down all your work and start over.

While tearing down work that was done without a permit may seem a good punishment by a city administrator, it is a needless waste of resources if the work was done right. In such a situation you should be able to compromise, such as by getting an architect to examine your work and provide plans after the fact for what you have done. If the department insists that the work must be torn down (and it is not defective), it would be worth appealing this decision to a higher authority.

HOME BUSINESSES

For most of human history, people worked from their homes. Blacksmiths worked from their garages, lawyers from their home office, and artists in their back yard. In the last century that has changed. In most residential communities work is forbidden. Today we have workplaces and residential areas. There are laws to keep them from mixing.

With technology allowing more people to perform valuable services in small clean work areas, and with parents wanting to both work and care for their children, the issue of the legality of home businesses comes up often.

In some areas, only troublesome businesses are illegal. Some examples, are contractors who keep all their equipment in their yards. People who have truck deliveries several times a day. Hairdressers, accountants, and lawyers who have clients coming to the house all day.

But in other areas, even sitting home and making business phone calls is illegal.

Example 1: The New Hampshire Supreme Court ruled that a roofing contractor could not work out of his home making phone calls and sending letters.

Example 2: The Massachusetts Supreme Court allowed a man to make phone calls and pay bills for his business, only because he did not keep a filing cabinet in the room.

Whether a home business is legal depends on the wording of the zoning ordinance. Many ordinances allow *accessory uses* of the property in residential zones. Some allow specific uses. Others only forbid specific businesses. But many forbid any business activities at all, such as keeping a collection of old books that are offered for sale. In some areas, violation of these laws is a criminal offense.

However, the state of the law does not reflect the reality in America today. It is estimated that over 20 million Americans run businesses out of their homes. Considering the difficulty of counting such small enterprises, the number is probably much greater. The online marketplace, Ebay, added millions of businesses in the last few years.

Zoning Regulations and Your Home Business

What is a home business owner to do if the zoning law forbids his business? The four choices are to:

   ◆ change the law;
   ◆ ignore the law;
   ◆ rent commercial space; or,
   ◆ move.

Change the law. Many cities are changing their zoning laws to accommodate home businesses. Yours may be ripe for a proposal to change. There are good arguments that today home businesses do not affect the neighborhood adversely. They can lower crime rates since more people are home during the day. They also allow those formerly on government assistance to begin earning money without needing capital for commercial space

If you can't change the zoning law through the legislative process, you may be able to do so in court. This could be a much more expensive endeavor unless you get several others or an advocacy group to join you.

When a law no longer reflects the realities of society, it is a good time for courts to step in and change them. Depending on the wording of your state constitution, a court might rule that a law prohibiting a harmless activity such as making business phone calls is protected by your right to privacy.

Ignore the law. If you don't want to campaign for a new zoning law or file a court case challenging it, you can do what tens of millions of other Americans are doing, just quietly work in your home hoping the zoning authorities won't notice you. One disturbing fact about zoning enforcement is that it is usually based on complaints by neighbors. Zoning officials aren't allowed to check inside your house every year to see how you are using it, so the only way they know is if someone complains.

Complaints are usually based on visible storage of business equipment or unusual numbers of deliveries to the home. However, they can also be sparked by a jealous neighbor after you brag about your successful business.

Rent commercial space or move. If you are cited for operating a business out of your home, your options are usually to rent commercial space elsewhere or to move to another home. In some situations you may be able to merely rent a storage facility and still run some functions out of your home. (For more detailed information on how to contest a zoning decision, see the section on zoning at the end of this chapter.)

JAILS AND PRISONS

Jails and prisons being operated by the government, do not usually violate other laws such as zoning ordinances. However, if operated improperly, they may constitute a nuisance. In such cases, court action by the neighbors may be able to remedy the situation.

🏠 *A woman was living in a nice home on one of the most desirable streets in Vincennes, Indiana, when the county built a jail thirty feet away. It was a large jail that held an average of forty prisoners. The prison was also used to house the insane. At times the prisoners would look down into her home and "loudly scream, sing, swear, curse, and utter profane and indecent language." They would also pound on the bars and make loud and dismal noises. She sued, but the court held that the owner of a residence has no remedy for an injury from a properly built jail conducted in a proper manner. It said the noise from the jail was unavoidable and that the county has a duty to house criminals and the insane somewhere. It did concede, however, that allowing the prisoners to look into her residence was an invasion of her privacy and that the sheriff and the jailer may be liable for that.*

🏠 *The Board of County Commissioners of Baldwin County, Georgia, decided to build a convict camp north of the city of Milledgeville. The residents of a nearby subdivision went to court to try to get an injunction against building the camp. The court declined to issue the injunction and the Supreme Court of Georgia agreed, saying that a prison or convict camp was not a nuisance unless it was not operated properly. It could not be stopped before it was built.*

🏠 *A man filed suit against the North Carolina State Prison Commission to force them to stop allowing criminals to wander the streets and to halt construction of an expansion to the Camp Polk Prison northwest of Raleigh. The judge noted that escapees and discharged prisoners committed serious crimes in the area and issued the injunction.*

In this case, however, the victory was short-lived as the North Carolina Supreme Court dissolved the injunction because the man had failed to allege that the prison commission had acted fraudulently or in an arbitrary manner. In addition, he had found no ordinance prohibiting prisons in the area.

TREES

Throughout the country, municipalities are enacting ordinances protecting trees. Not trees the municipalities own on public land, but trees its residents own. These laws typically forbid a property owner from cutting down his own tree, on his own property, unless he gets a permit. He then must either replace it with a tree of equal size or pay the municipality a fee amounting to as much as $35 to $100 an inch.

Considering that the constitution forbids the state from taking a person's property without paying for it, it is hard to understand how the government can make a citizen pay for taking his own tree. Doesn't this mean that the government has taken ownership of all trees on private property?

While many Americans think that their property rights should be *sacrosanct*, many more apparently feel that their right to enjoy their neighbors' trees is even more important. Thus, tree ordinances are being passed in more places with harsher fines. A recent inquiry from a Florida city to the state attorney general was whether they could set their fine at $12,500.

People have spent months in jail and been fined tens of thousands of dollars for disobeying tree ordinances.

> **Example 1:** A man in Arlington County, Virginia was jailed for over three months and fined $48,000 for not planting enough trees on his property. He had followed the instructions of one city employee, but her replacement wanted them in other locations.

Example 2: (But some people have fought these laws and won.) A later victim of the Arlington County tree ordinance had it declared unconstitutional and was awarded a cash settlement against the county.

🏠 *In Northbrook, Illinois, a homeowner asked for a hardship variance to cut down a tree so he could use a special van for his handicapped child. The town refused. Its attorney said that a legal hardship is one related to the character of the land (such as being unable to build around a tree), not the owners, since their ownership of the land is temporary.*

Preservation Ordinances

Since tree preservation ordinances are relatively recent, there have not been a lot of court cases on them. However, the few cases have gone both ways, some upholding the ordinances and others rejecting them as unconstitutional.

One argument against ordinances is that by penalizing a property owner for cutting down his own tree, the government has changed his ownership of property from *absolute* to *life estate*. That is, the owner is now considered only as the caretaker of the land for his life for the benefit of the community. This would be a *taking of an owner's property right*.

Tree ordinances are often part of zoning ordinances. Even if they are not, they are usually analyzed in the same way. If you wish to fight a tree ordinance, be sure to review the material in the next section on zoning laws.

ZONING

Zoning disputes are some of the most common problems homeowners have with government. But as usual, the government is not always right. There are many ways you can win a zoning dispute with the government.

While there were some land-use controls early in our nation's history, widespread zoning laws did not begin until the early 1900s. Previously, cities were a mix of shops, factories, and homes. These laws attempted to segregate these activities into zones and limit what could be done in each zone.

The good side of zoning is that a property owner knows that his neighbors can't do anything that is not allowed by the zoning and might lower the value of his property. The bad side of zoning is that the property owner can't do what he wants with his own property, if it does not comply with the zoning.

Controlling what everyone in the city can do with their land resulted in many court cases. The first big zoning case to come before the United States Supreme Court involved the city of Euclid, Ohio, in 1926. In this case, the city had set aside districts where no businesses were allowed. A company argued that it was not fair to forbid all businesses, since some businesses are quiet and do not disturb the neighborhood. It said that lowering the value of its property by limiting what it could build on it was an unconstitutional taking of the value of that property.

The Supreme Court disagreed, saying that zoning was a legitimate government power when properly used and that—

before the ordinance can be declared unconstitutional, it must be proven that such provisions are clearly arbitrary and unreasonable, having no substantial relation to the public health, safety, morals, or general welfare.

Over the years there have been thousands of cases challenging zoning laws. If you have a dispute regarding your zoning, most likely you can find a case nearly identical to yours. However, each state's zoning laws are different. The zoning ordinances passed by municipalities under these laws are also different. Check your own state's court cases for the best guidance. In cases where zoning violates the federal Constitution, then federal court decisions including the United States Supreme Court may provide the answer.

Regulations Determined by Situation Basis

One problem with zoning, from the beginning, was that it was hap-
hazard. Challenges to zoning regulations were decided by judges
looking at individual situations. Considering how politics works in
both large and small cities, it is not surprising that a lot of zoning
was decided by political connections, rather than a greater good.

But as more cases reached the high courts of the states, the idea
that comprehensive plans should be used was adopted. The current
situation in most areas is that if there is a reasonable comprehensive
plan, the zoning is valid unless it violates a constitutional right such
as a taking of property or equal protection. If it does not, judges are
not allowed to change it because making zoning decisions is a legislative task, not a judicial one.

A major question about zoning has been whether it served a
legitimate state purpose. Originally, zoning was only supposed to
protect people's health and welfare. Zoning that merely made a city
look prettier was invalid. But today, more and more types of zoning
controls are being held valid. Governments are being given more
power over private property as judges decide that aesthetically-
pleasing communities are necessary for citizens' health and welfare.

There are two ways to attack zoning.

Apply for administrative review. This means filing an appeal
with the next higher lever of authority in the zoning system.

Ask for judicial review. This means filing a court case against the
zoning board. Usually this would be done in state court, but if your
constitutional rights have been violated you might be able to sue in
federal court.

Violation of Fifth Amendment

Another major issue of zoning is whether it takes the value of property in violation of the Fifth Amendment requiring that citizens be
paid when their property is taken. The general issue that the government may zone property for different uses (giving more value to
some property and taking some value from other property) has been
long-settled. But when zoning takes all the value from property or

when it forces a property owner to bear the cost of a benefit to the public unrelated to his property, this can be an unconstitutional taking of his property rights.

Example 1: The United States Supreme Court ruled that when an oceanfront property owner in South Carolina was forbidden from building anything on his lots, this was a *taking* by the state that must be paid for.

Example: 2: In another case, the Supreme Court ruled that when the California Coastal Commission told a property owner she could not get a permit to remodel her property unless she gave them an easement over her beach front, it was a *taking of her property*. In fact, the beach easement was unrelated to the remodeling.

THE GOVERNMENT

There are many groups dedicated to helping people who have problems with the government. Below are the web sites for a few of them.

American Association of Small Property Owners
www.smallpropertyowner.com

American Land Rights Association
www.landrights.org

Defenders of Property Rights
www.yourpropertyrights.org

Pacific Legal Foundation
www.pacificlegal.org

Property Rights Congress of America, Inc.
www.freedom.org/prc/
Sovereignty International
http://sovereignty.freedom.org

United Property Owners
www.unitedpropertyowners.org

CHECKLIST:

GROUNDS FOR FIGHTING A ZONING DECISION

If any of these issues apply to your situation, do some further research or consult an attorney to see if your situation is actually a violation of your current state law.

☐ **Was the zoning law validly enacted?**

Cities are only allowed to enact zoning laws to the extent that a state statute gives them the power. Did the city follow all requirements of the statute? Does the zoning law comply with the state statute in all respects? Did you have reasonable notice of the enactment of the zoning?

☐ **Is the zoning law valid as it applies to you?**

Does it relate to a valid purpose such as health and safety? Or is its purpose invalid in your state, such as aesthetics?

☐ **Is the zoning arbitrary or unreasonable?**

Is it spot zoning? Is it unrelated to the character of the neighborhood? Is the zoning of the property rationally related to the goal the city is trying to achieve? Is the burden on your property reasonably related to the benefit to the public?

☐ **Is the zoning of your property inconsistent with the comprehensive plan?**

Is your property treated similarly to similar properties? Is the law indefinite, vague, or uncertain? Does it give too much discretion to the enforcement personnel? Are there clear guidelines determined by the legislative authority?

☐ **Is the zoning confiscatory?**

Does it take away all or most of the value of your property?

☐ **Was the zoning authority unconstitutionally delegated?**
Are zoning decisions left to parties who aren't legally entitled to them, such as an enforcement officer?

☐ **Is the treatment of your property the same as similar properties?**
Is your property the only one in the area with lower use potential than surrounding properties?

☐ **Were any of your vested rights taken by the zoning?**
Was the zoning changed after you received a permit to improve it? Did a government body lead you to believe you had some rights before you took action in reliance on those rights?

—9—
TAKING YOUR DISPUTE TO COURT

Going to court should be the last thing you consider to solve a neighbor dispute. (Moving away could be cheaper and easier.)

A civil court action is the most expensive and slowest way to stop a neighbor problem, but it can be very effective. Sometimes just the threat of a suit can convince your neighbor to solve the problem. With most lawyer's fees now in the $100 to $200 an hour range, a dispute that ends up in court can easily cost $10,000. A neighbor who gets a letter from your lawyer and checks with his own lawyer may decide that annoying you is not worth the price.

In most cases, a neighbor dispute isn't the kind of case a lawyer will take on a *contingency basis* (meaning that you don't pay anything; the lawyer collects a percentage *only* after the case is won). Because neighbor disputes involve high emotions and can drag on indefinitely, most lawyers won't even give you a fixed price to take such a case. Also, most lawyers will want to be paid by the hour for all work needed to be done.

Once a case is filed, the lawyer's meter starts running. If the other side sets a hearing, your lawyer has to do research, prepare documents, and appear in court. That may be ten hours of work. If the other side sets a deposition of a dozen of the surrounding neighbors, that may take two weeks of eight hour days.

If several neighbors are confronted with one problem neighbor, the costs may be greatly reduced by agreeing to share the costs of the suit. Meanwhile, the problem neighbor will have to pay his fees, himself.

SMALL CLAIMS COURT

In some cases, you may be able to bring an action against a neighbor in *small claims court*. This is a court where you do not need a lawyer, so it can be an inexpensive way to solve your dispute.

In most states you can use a lawyer in small claims court if you wish, but in others lawyers are not allowed. (Check with the clerk of your small claims court to determine if you can use an attorney in that court, if you wish.)

If you sue someone in small claims court and he or she hires a lawyer to counter-sue, definitely get advice from a lawyer on how to proceed. If your opponent has a lawyer, you *may* be at a great disadvantage in the case without one to present your side.

Depending upon which state you live in, the maximum amount of your claim may be limited to $1,500, or as much as $25,000. In some states, you may request *equitable relief*, such as a court order that the neighbor stop doing something. However, in many states, small claims courts cannot give equitable relief. They can only award a sum of money for damages.

If a court can only give damages and not order a person to stop something, it is possible they will pay the money and keep on doing it. This is especially true if it is a business that is making a good profit. (Keep in mind that if you win damages from a neighbor and the activity continues after the lawsuit, you can sue again for additional damages.)

SMALL CLAIMS COURT LIMITS

Alabama	$3,000
Alaska	$7,500
Arizona	$2,500
Arkansas	$5,000
California	$5,000
Colorado	$7,500
Connecticut	$3,500
Delaware	$15,000
District of Columbia	$5,000
Florida	$5,000

Georgia	$15,000
Hawaii	$3,500
Idaho	$4,000
Illinois	$5,000
	(Cook County—$1,500)
Indiana	$3,000
	(Marion and Allen Counties—$6,000)
Iowa	$5,000
Kansas	$1,800
Kentucky	$1,500
Louisiana	$3,000
Maine	$4,500
Maryland	$2,500
Massachusetts	$2,000
Michigan	$3,000
Minnesota	$7,500
Mississippi	$2,500
Missouri	$3,000
Montana	$3,000
Nebraska	$2,400
Nevada	$5,000
New Hampshire	$5,000
New Jersey	$3,000
New Mexico	$10,000
New York	$3,000
North Carolina	$4,000
North Dakota	$5,000
Ohio	$3,000
Oklahoma	$4,500
Oregon	$5,000
Pennsylvania	$8,000
Rhode Island	$1,500
South Carolina	$7,500
South Dakota	$8,000
Tennessee	$15,000
	(Shelby and Anderson Counties—$25,000)

Texas	$5,000
Utah	$5,000
Vermont	$3,500
Virginia	$2,000
Washington	$4,000
West Virginia	$5,000
Wisconsin	$5,000
Wyoming	$3,000

NUISANCE LAW

The law that would usually be used in a civil court case over a neighbor dispute is a *nuisance law*. This is a collection of court cases developed over hundreds of years of deciding disputes. Most of the cases are from your state and perhaps your district, but a court could consider cases from other states if they help analyze the situation.

In the colloquial sense, the word nuisance can describe anything annoying. But when an activity is so annoying that it warrants court action, it is called an *actionable nuisance*. For a nuisance to be actionable, the following three elements must be present:

- ◆ a legal right;
- ◆ an invasion of that right; and,
- ◆ an injury.

The *legal right* in most cases is the right to quiet enjoyment of one's property. However, American courts have recognized that people are not entitled to absolute silence. The *level of annoyance* before a nuisance becomes actionable depends upon the time and the place. One court has said that it is important to note "the ordinary comfort of human existence as understood by the American people in their present state of enlightenment."

A comment to the Restatement of Torts (a summary of the state of the law), states—

Each individual in a community must put up with a certain amount of annoyance, inconvenience and interference, and must take a certain amount of risk in order that all may get on together.

🏠 *In Bridgewater, Massachusetts in 1905, a person had a hen house near enough to another dwelling that the owner claimed it made it difficult to rent. However, the court held that poultry odors were not offensive to an ordinary citizen of Massachusetts. The fact that a person is sensitive to the activity that is complained of does not matter. The law in America is that if some people are more sensitive than others, they should move to a suitable location; not expect others to change their lifestyle.*

🏠 *A man who suffered from sunstroke and congestion of the brain was living across the street from a church in Provincetown, Massachusetts. Whenever the bell was rung, he would go into convulsions that could cause his death. The bell ringer at the church was asked to stop, but that just made him want to ring the bell even more. He said that he would not stop for any reason, much less for the man who complained. He added that if it would kill him, he would still keep it up. (It seems the man had previously had the bell ringer arrested for battery.) The court decided that since the man was an unusually sensitive person and that an ordinary person would not be disturbed by the bell, it was not a nuisance.*

The *invasion of the right to quiet enjoyment of one's property* can include many types of things. Noises, odors, vibrations, heat, smoke, flooding, and keeping explosives. But it is required that the harm caused by an action must be substantial for it to be deemed a nuisance. One of the author's favorite Latin maxims (and one of the few he remembers) is *de minimis non curat lex*, the law will not concern itself with trifles.

Courts have not been sympathetic in cases in which the only damage claimed was the loss of property value. As the Court of Appeals of Kentucky once explained it—

It is fundamental that a buyer of property assumes the risk of changing community conditions. Sometimes the value of his property is enhanced, and he does not have to pay for the enhancement. Sometimes it declines and he has no recourse. These facts of life are not subject to an exception simply because the source of the transition can be identified and is suable.

FILING A LAWSUIT

One basic aspect of *nuisance and trespass law* is that it is tied to the ownership of real property. In its usual sense a nuisance is when one person uses his property in a way that affects another's use of his own property. A common example of this is someone diverting water on his own property that causes a flood on another's property. However, the definition has been expanded over the years to broadly define the term *use of property*. Thus, a person who keeps a barking dog can be held to be using his property to cause a nuisance on another's property.

Since nuisance law regards interests in property, only persons who have some legal interest in property can take court action. Persons such as employees and guests cannot use nuisance law to protect themselves. However, the complainant need not actually own the land, he can be a renter, own merely an easement on the land, or have another interest in the land.

🏠 *Twenty employees in the yard of a railroad company in Jacksonville, Florida, filed a suit for nuisance because they were bothered by fumes, dust, and gasses from the neighboring chemical company. However, their suit was dismissed because they were employees, not owners or renters of the land. (This was in the days before pollution laws. Today a government agency would probably stop the fumes.)*

HOLDING SOMEONE LIABLE

There is a lawyers' rule that when there is an incident—sue everyone in sight. The logic is that you never know what a jury will decide. Some parties may make some payment to settle the case, just because it is cheaper than paying an attorney to fight it. However, this rule is changing. In some states and in all federal courts, there are rules if you file a frivolous lawsuit; you may have to pay the other side's attorney fees. You may also have to pay a penalty known as *sanctions*.

In order to file a lawsuit against someone, you should have at least an arguable case. There should be some legal argument for holding the person liable and some proof that the person is in some way at fault.

You should sue everyone against whom you have evidence and an arguable case. Your case can also be dismissed if you leave out a party who is a *necessary party* to a suit. A necessary party is one whose actions are so much a part of the case that it cannot be fairly decided without him or her present. For example, if someone damaged your trees and you sue the power company who employed him, you will probably need to sue the actual person who did the damage. That person will need to testify as to what he did and why he did it.

NOTE: *If you have any doubts, consult an attorney and get an expert opinion as to whom you should sue.*

🏠 *A man was walking down the street in Birmingham, Alabama. At that time, "a piece of rock or other foreign substance was blown, blasted, thrown, or caused to fall upon or against" him, causing his shoulder, collar bone, ribs and various other bones to be broken, and causing him to be "mashed, bruised, strained, sprained and otherwise injured in various parts of his person." He sued several parties for damages, including the iron and railroad company, the owner of the land where the blasting*

was taking place. After reviewing the facts of the case,
the court held that the owner of the land where the blast-
ing took place was not liable, since it had leased the land
to the other parties who had control over the blasting
operations.

POSSIBLE COURT FINDINGS

There are two types of relief a court can usually grant in a neighbor dispute: *monetary damages* or an *injunction*.

Monetary Damages

In most cases, the monetary damages awarded for a nuisance are *actual damages.* Those are the actual amounts necessary to compensate you for the loss caused by the nuisance or trespass. This may be the loss of rental value of the property if the nuisance is *temporary* or the loss of market value of the property if the nuisance is *perma-nent.* If there has been some physical damage to another piece of property, the damages may be the cost of restoring it.

In some cases where there are no actual damages, such as someone trespassing in your yard, you could get nominal damages, such as a dollar. In other cases, where actual or nominal damages are inadequate, a court might award *special damages.* An example of this would be where a nuisance makes a farm useless for farming, but does not lower its value. The question in this type of situation is what would be fair compensation for the trouble, annoyance, and anxiety of having to move from one's lifelong home.

Where the person acted deliberately and maliciously, you might be able to get *punitive damages.* This remedy is usually only available where the party did something especially shocking to the court. Punitive damages are only available in a case where the complaining party has been held to be entitled, first, to actual or *nominal damages.*

In some states, there are statutes that specifically allow for punitive damages in certain cases. For instance, the state of Louisiana allows *triple damages* for cutting down another's trees without permission.

Injunctions

An *injunction* is a court order requiring the other party to take some action or to refrain from taking some action. Courts are usually reluctant to issue injunctions. However, in neighbor cases, there is a better than usual chance of obtaining an injunction, because the case usually involves land. Each piece of land is considered unique. The injunction can tell the other party to stop the activity completely or it can tell him to conduct it in a different manner. In some cases, courts have ordered the installation of noise suppression equipment and have ordered activities to be conducted only during certain hours of the day.

In nuisance and trespass lawsuits, attorney's fees are rarely awarded to the winner. This means that any amounts won will be reduced by the amounts owed to your attorney. Considering the thousands of dollars a suit would cost, going to court is not worth it for small sums. And the cost of an injunction, even if you win, will be substantial.

In some cases, there is some kind of written agreement between the parties indicating how attorney's fees may be awarded. For instance, a lease between a landlord and tenant or a condominium declaration may provide that in suits between the parties, attorney fees must be paid by the losing party.

> *A cooperative apartment association filed suit against a tenant to force her to obey the rules of the building. The rules included such issues as dressing appropriately in the lobby, using the right door to the pool, and, requiring her to supply them with an access key to her apartment.*

In this case, after five years of litigation involving several lawsuits, the tenant was awarded $87,375.00 in attorney's fees.

WEIGHING THE RIGHTS OF BOTH SIDES

When a court is faced with a case involving an alleged nuisance, it must weigh the rights of the two sides and come to a decision which is as equitable as possible. A person awakened by a neighbor who must practice the trumpet may feel his rights are being violated, but the trumpet player also feels he has rights to use his property as he wishes. In striking a balance between the competing interests, the courts will look at several factors.

With nuisance, as with many areas of the law, the court will look to what is *reasonable*. There has long been a *reasonable man standard* (more recently renamed the *reasonable person standard*) to decide whether conduct is allowable. In nuisance cases, there is also an examination of the gravity of the harm versus the utility of the enterprise. In other words, the court will see if the person alleged to be creating a nuisance is doing more harm than good.

In examining the gravity of the harm and the utility of the enterprise, the court will look at: the type of harm being caused to the person complaining; the social value of what the person is doing; the suitability of what he is doing in the location; and, the burden on him to avoid the problem himself.

More recently, courts have looked at whether it would be possible to compensate neighbors for the harm and loss of value of their property.

> **Example:** A cement company had a factory that cost $45 million, paid substantial taxes, and employed 300 people. It had done everything feasible to keep its operation clean and quiet, but was still causing problems for its neighbors. The court held that it would not be reasonable to stop the operation completely, so it ordered that the company pay $185,000 to the people who were bothered by the operation to compensate them for the problems. This payment would be considered a payment for the lost value of their property and would be a one-time payment. (A future purchaser of the property could not sue for

damages since he should have, theoretically, paid a reduced price for the land.)

POTENTIAL DEFENSES

When a person is sued for nuisance, the burden will be upon the person filing the suit to prove that there was an actionable nuisance and that the person being sued caused it. If this is not proven, then the case should be dismissed. Even if it is proven, the person sued may have some defenses that justify the action.

Statutes of Limitations

Laws that determine specific limits of the time period in which you can file a suit for a certain type of action are called *statutes of limitations*. For instance, the time limit may be one year to file a suit for encroachments on your property if they are under six inches. Check state statutes thoroughly for limitations. The limitation for something such as simple trespass may be one time period, such as five years, but another statute may apply to certain types of trespass and be two years or longer.

Consent

If a person consents to your action, he or she cannot sue you unless the consent was withdrawn prior to your action. For instance, if your neighbor says you can walk through his yard, he cannot sue you for trespass if you do. If you are bitten by his dog, he cannot use trespass as a defense to your suit over the dog bite.

Sometimes consent can be presumed. For instance, a person ordering a pizza can be assumed to have granted the delivery person permission to enter his property for the purpose of delivering the pizza.

Self-Defense

If you must take some action to protect yourself or your property, then in many cases this is a defense to a suit. For instance, if your neighbor' sprinkler is spraying water onto your porch and ruining your furniture, you could go on his property and redirect it without risk of being guilty of trespass (unless in moving the sprinkler you cause damage to the neighbor's property).

Defense of Others

Similarly, defending someone else from injury can be a defense to a lawsuit. If your neighbor's pit bull attacks a child walking down the street, you can beat the dog, if that is the only reasonable way to stop it from injuring the child.

Contributory Negligence

Ordinarily, nuisance does not involve negligence, so *contributory negligence* is rarely a factor considered. But occasionally, nuisance and negligence overlap and the distinction between the two is not clear. Courts will sometimes confuse the two and call something negligent a nuisance or vice versa.

> While stepping from a driveway to a sidewalk in Niagara Falls, New York, in the 1920s, a woman caught her heel and stumbled. She sued the city for negligence, saying that the condition of the area was a nuisance. The court held that the condition could be a nuisance, but that the jury could consider if she had also been negligent when she fell.

Assumption of the Risk

In some cases, a person's actions indicate that he consciously decided to assume the risk, waiving the right to sue. For instance, if you go sledding down your neighbor's hill and break your leg, a court could rule that you assumed the risk and that your neighbor had done nothing wrong.

Legislative Authority

Just as the legislature can make an activity illegal, it can make it lawful. When a city zones a certain area for heavy industry, the city gives authority to occupiers of that land to engage in industrial activities. Activities that might be a nuisance in another area, can be legal in an industrial area.

Variance

If some activity is against a zoning law, it may be possible to be granted a *variance* or a special exception to the law.

Nonconforming Use

If a property is being used a certain way when a zoning law is passed, in most cases the use will be allowed to continue. In such cases, we say the use was *grandfathered in*. If the use is not allowed to continue, then the law will probably be held unconstitutional as a taking of property without compensation. (Some courts have allowed a use to be phased out through amortization over a number of years.)

Legalized Nuisance

Even if a court finds some activity to be a nuisance, a legislative body may later make it legal.

> ***Example:*** A bell manufacturer in Plymouth, Massachusetts had been restrained by a court from ringing a bell on his mill before the hour of 6:30 a.m. Several years later, the legislature passed an act that allowed manufacturers and employers to ring bells, gongs, and whistles in order to give notice to employees at times the towns could designate. Plymouth allowed the bell ringing to begin at 5 a.m., and the bell manufacturer asked the court to lift the injunction from ringing before 6:30 a.m. The person who had originally sued him claimed the statute was unconstitutional. The court held the statute constitutional and that since the manufacturer had taken the proper procedures, he was entitled to ring his bell.

Right to Farm Laws

In some states there are *right to farm laws* that protect farmers from nuisance suits. These are useful to farmers as subdivisions are built closer and closer to farms. The subdivision residents are often annoyed by the smells or noises coming from the farms.

Moving to the Nuisance

If a person has been engaging in an activity for a number of years and another person moves nearby and objects to the activity, the person who was there first may have the greater right. As discussed previously, many factors will be taken into account, such as the character of the locale and the amount of disturbance being created. (If the activity is *unreasonable*, however, it is unlikely that the person creating the nuisance will be able to continue, just because he got there first.

> *There was a road on the southern slope of Red Mountain in Birmingham, Alabama. It was an exclusive, residential area. The nearby railroad tracks of the Louisville & Nashville Railroad Co. had not been in use for some time. But during the war, the railroad was needed for nearby coal mines and other operations. These operations caused dust and smoke, loud noises from the beating of the rail cars to empty them, and odors and fumes. Some residents filed suit against the railroad and others in an attempt to abate the nuisance.*

In this case, the issue reached the Alabama Supreme Court. It held that while some of the noise and fumes were unnecessary and must be reduced, the residents could not stop the lawful operation of the railroad that had been there first.

> *When a corporation began its cattle feeding operations in Maricopa County, Arizona, it was far from the edge of any city. However, a real estate development company decided this was a good area for its Sun City retirement*

community and purchased land nearby to create its com-
munity. Because the odors, flies, and other annoyances
of the cattle feeding lot would make the community less
attractive to potential residents, the developer sued to
have the operations stopped.

In this case, the Arizona Supreme Court, in balancing the rights of the parties, decided that it would order the cattle feed lot to stop operations, but that the developer would have to pay all costs of moving or shutting down the operation.

Acts of Others

The fact that others are also creating a nuisance is not a defense to one charged with nuisance. But if an area is predominantly industrial or commercial, then others in the area will have less right to complain about noise, smoke, or smells than if it was a residential area.

Prescriptive Right

A *prescriptive right* is a right that is acquired through continued use. Although it has been held that one may not acquire a prescriptive right to maintain a *public nuisance*, there have been cases that have found a prescriptive right to take action that might otherwise constitute a *private nuisance*.

Laches

Laches means that a person has not enforced his right for a considerable length of time. In some cases, failing to object may constitute acquiescence and a person may lose his right to object in the future. However, failing to object when a nuisance is slight does not preclude one from objecting when it becomes greater.

🏠 *Some people started building greenhouses on their land*
in Northumberland County, Pennsylvania, near the land
eventually owned by Susquehanna Collieries Co. In the
operation of its coal business, the company washed,

sifted rock and coal, and piled it on their land. When it dried, the dust blew onto the greenhouses, spotting the plants, pitting the glass, and causing other problems. Years later, the owners complained a couple times about the problem, but it wasn't until another eight years had passed that they filed suit. The court held that under the doctrine of laches, they had waited too long to seek an injunction, but that they might be able to sue for monetary damages.

After becoming blind, a man purchased a home with his wife on Butler Street in Pittsburgh, Pennsylvania, in a mixed residential and manufacturing district. Later his wife died and he owned the home himself. American Spiral Spring & Manufacturing Company purchased the lot behind his home to build a manufacturing plant. They contacted him and told him the plant would be noisy and offered to buy his property. He refused to sell.

In this case, they then opened their plant and placed the noisiest equipment closest to his home. He complained, but they only offered to purchase his property at the value of the land with no payment for the building. Fourteen months later he sued.

At trial it was shown that the vibrations were so bad that pictures and plaster shook from the walls and articles bounced off tables. The company contended that because he waited fourteen months, he was precluded from complaining about the noise. The court disagreed and said that the heavy machinery would have to be moved away from his house, even though moving it would cost more than the house was worth.

Emergency
In an emergency situation such as a war, a nuisance may be allowed to continue when the court weighs the equities.

🏠 *In New Jersey, the electric company was using the best equipment available at the time, but it still caused fly ash, dirt, soot, dust, and cinders in the neighborhood. The neighbors sued and the court held that during the war nothing would be done, but the neighbors could refile their suit after the war.*

🏠 *Mt. Vernon Die Casting Corp. on 242nd Street in Bronx, N.Y. was causing a nuisance for a neighbor who owned rental property. In a lawsuit, the court held that during the war, the company had to pay the owner of the property the amount by which his property was lowered in rental value. After the war it would have to stop the nuisance.*

Prevention of disease. In some cases an effort to prevent the spread of a disease can constitute an emergency grave enough to be a defense to a court action.

🏠 *To prevent the further spread of a smallpox epidemic, the city of Knoxville had the hospital beds, sheets, and clothing of infected patients burned once the patient left the hospital. The state brought suit claiming that the burning of the infected material infected and poisoned the atmosphere around the highways and homes of citizens near the hospital. The state claimed the air was so corrupt and unhealthy it was a nuisance.*

In this case, the court held the act was done by public authority for public safety to prevent the spread of disease. The court held the burnings were done with reasonable care and with a regard for safety. It said this was a temporary inconvenience that was justified under the circumstances and the state could not enforce criminal liability.

Environmental Laws

There are many recently-enacted environmental laws that change neighbor's rights. For example, there are now laws that say people can put up clotheslines (to save energy) or may install solar heating devices. These laws often say they overrule local laws and property restrictions.

NOTE: *Finding laws like these might not be easy. They are often buried in a law with an unrelated title and the index to your state's statutes might not be thorough. Carefully go through the statutes to see what you can find, if you are evaluating an environmental concern.*

If you have something on your property that your neighbors are complaining about, check the statutes and see if it is allowed in spite of a local zoning law or restriction. If you want to get rid of something your neighbor has and he is using a law like this to justify it, check with a lawyer to see if there is a way to challenge the law. There may be procedural or constitutional problems with the law that could invalidate it.

LEGALLY RELEVANT DEFENSES

In both civil and criminal cases, people sometimes come into court with perfectly good sounding excuses why they did or didn't do something. But often the excuse is not a *legal defense*. That is, their excuse is not *legally relevant* to the issue. Each area of law considers some issues relevant and others irrelevant. If you do not address the relevant issues, you cannot win your case—no matter how right you are on the irrelevant issues.

The following are examples of some defenses that didn't work. (Keep in mind that the law is different in every jurisdiction and these cases might not be followed precisely in your area.)

Benefit

It is irrelevant that the activity complained of increases the value of the property owned by the persons complaining.

Example: Some people in Prairie City, Oregon sued a neighbor who had set up a drain over her property to carry away water from a septic tank. The neighbor argued that having the drain on her property was a benefit to the others. However, the Supreme Court of Oregon ruled that a person can never justify a trespass by showing a benefit to the owner of the land.

Unable to Afford

The inability to afford a remedy to a nuisance is not a legal defense to a nuisance action.

Example: The Baltimore & Yorktown Turnpike Rd. was indicted for maintaining a public nuisance when it allowed its road to fall into a ruinous and defective condition. The road authority contended that it did not have the money to pay for repairs. The court held that this was not a defense to the *criminal charge.*

No Other Place to Do It

A person's claim that he has no other place to conduct the activity is not a legal defense.

Example: In Portland, Maine, a family was running business on their property. This activity caused noxious odors, filth, and noises that disturbed the neighbors. The state brought an action for nuisance. The family argued that they had no place else to do the work. The court ruled that this was not a legal defense.

State-Approved Activity

A license by the state to do an activity is not a defense to do it in a way that constitutes a nuisance.

Example: A sewage company in Camden, New Jersey was indicted for a criminal nuisance because of unpleasant odors from its plant. It defended itself on the grounds that it was operating under direction of the Board of Health, using plans of the State Sewage Commission. The courts said that was not a defense because the Board of Health could not authorize a nuisance.

Benefit to the Public
The fact that an activity benefits the public is not a defense if it is done in such a way as to constitute a nuisance.

Example: A resident of Warren County, Illinois was charged with criminal nuisance for operating a rendering plant (turning dead animals into various products) in close proximity to several residences. He argued that his business was a benefit to the public. However, the Supreme Court of Illinois held that this was not a defense to a charge of nuisance.

Plaintiff Failed to Abate
Persons injured by a nuisance do not have a legal duty to lessen their damages by moving away or avoiding the area.

Example: A gas plant in the city of Reton, Washington, was annoying the neighbors by allegedly emitting odors and discharging bothersome chemicals that injured the neighbors and damaged their house and some trees. A jury awarded $2,500 to the neighbors, but the verdict was set aside.

In a second trial, the jury awarded $500, but this was reversed by the appellate court because the trial judge erroneously told the jury that the neighbors had the duty to lessen their damages by moving from the premises.

The court ruled that in nuisance cases, a person does not have to minimize his own damages. Therefore the neighbors were allowed to conduct a third trial.

DETERMINING THE LAW

When students go to law school, they do not get books that tell them what the law is. They get books filled with cases and after reading these, they are supposed to figure out what the law is. However, after three years and thousands of cases, they come to the realization that no one knows what the law is.

Two cases look identical. The facts seem to be the same, but the results are completely opposite. For a hundred years, the results always went one way, but now in this case, the court says there is an exception because of some minor detail.

Some people say that the law is what the judge assigned to your case says it is. If the law is completely on your side and you have carefully covered your position in every way, but the judge gets the impression that you are dishonest and are taking advantage of an innocent person, you may still lose your case. There are exceptions to every rule. These exceptions were created so that a judge could reach the *right decision* at *that specific time*.

Proper Interpretation of the Law

The purpose of appeals courts is to review the holdings of the trial judges and to be sure that the law was properly interpreted and justly applied. Appeals courts do not see the parties or take any testimony. They just look at the written record of the case, listen to the lawyers' argument as to what law applies, and see if the law was properly applied by the trial judge. Supposedly, this insulates them from getting involved with the emotional or personal aspects of the parties.

DECIDING A COURT CASE

Most cases involve two types of questions: *questions of fact* and *questions of law*. Questions of fact may be decided by a jury or if a jury is waived, by a judge. These involve issues of what actually happened. Questions of fact are decided upon the evidence presented to the court, such as the testimony of the witnesses. Questions of fact cannot be appealed since litigants are usually allowed only one chance to present their evidence. Usually, the only way a litigant can get a second chance to present evidence is if there is some fundamental error in the trial and a new trial must be held.

Questions of law involve how the law applies to the facts that have been established. Questions of law are decided by the judge. These may be appealed if the judge makes a legal error. To make things even more complicated, sometimes a question can be either one of law or of fact.

An example explaining the difference between law and fact could be a theft. You charge your neighbor with taking your hose and he is charged with theft. The questions of fact for the jury would be whether it was your hose and whether your neighbor had it. If the jury agreed that it was your hose and that your neighbor did have it, it would then be a question of law for the judge as to whether this constituted a theft under the theft statute. If a neighborhood child took you hose and left it on your neighbor's lawn, or if your spouse loaned it to him the result would be different than if the neighbor went into your garage and took it.

With things like nuisances it is a bit more complicated. Suppose you are kept up every night by a loud noise that rattles your house and so you sue the factory next door. The questions of fact to be decided by the jury are: Were you actually kept awake by the noise? Was your house actually rattled? Was this caused by the factory? Assuming the jury decides that all these things are true, the next question would be whether these facts constitute a nuisance. Some courts have ruled that such question is a question of fact for the jury, but others have said it is a question of law. Once it is decided that there is a nuisance and that you are entitled to an injunction halting the noise plus monetary compensation for damage to your house, the amount of monetary damage would then be a question of fact for the jury.

POSSIBILITIES FOR COURTROOM SUCCESS

Of all the cases brought to lawyers, only a small percentage actually go to trial. Many are settled after negotiations; some are settled after a lawsuit is filed; and, a large number are settled just before or during the trial. The reason for this is that there is no way to predict the outcome of a trial.

No matter how strong the law is on your side, no matter how ideal your witnesses are, you can lose your case. Juries of six or twelve different individuals do not always act on logic. They do not always understand the instructions of the judge and they do not always believe the witnesses. Waiving a jury and leaving all the questions to the judge may result in a more logical decision, but it may not always be a better decision.

Everyone taking a matter to court has a 50% chance of winning or losing. Lawyers know there is no such thing as a sure case. Anything can happen in a lawsuit. Even if you have all the facts and the law is on your side—you can still lose. How can this happen? The judge may not believe you, he or she may misinterpret the law, or you may just end up looking like the *bad guy* after the other side tells their side of the case. This is why so many cases are settled out of court. For every case that goes to trial, many more are settled before trial—especially in the 24 hour period just before trial.

Keep this in mind when deciding how to handle your case. If you can get the other side to make a reasonable offer—take it. If you can get part of what you want, compare it to losing the case completely. Don't be greedy. Don't try to teach him a lesson. Don't just try to get even. You might end up losing.

–10–
RESEARCHING YOUR CASE

Because of the wide scope of material covered in this book, only general principles can be explained and only a few cases can be given as examples. Many of the subjects in this book are thoroughly researched and explained in thousands of pages of articles and cases.

USING A LAW LIBRARY

If you have a specific problem that you would like to research further, you can find the information in a local law library or a larger public library. Many county courthouses have law libraries and many law school libraries are open to the public.

State Legal Encyclopedia

The best place to find information about the current state of the law in your state on any subject is a *state legal encyclopedia*. Unfortunately, such encyclopedias are not available for every state. They have only been published for California, Florida, Illinois, Maryland, Michigan, New York, Ohio, Pennsylvania and Texas.

American Law Reporters

The best place to find information about a specific problem is in the *American Law Reports* and they are abbreviated A.L.R. There are four series of these books They contain lengthy articles explaining, in detail, the state of the law on very specific topics such as crowds being nuisances or fence problems.

National Legal Encyclopedias

If there is no legal encyclopedia for your state and no article in any of the A.L.R.s, then check a national legal encyclopedia called *Corpus Juris Secundum* or C.J.S. This is a set of over 100, three-inch thick, blue books on every conceivable subject. Each subject is thoroughly analyzed and the cases from around the country noted by state in the footnotes. Sometimes a page may have one line of text and the rest footnotes.

When using any of these books, be sure to check inside the back cover for the *pocket part*. This is a supplement of recent laws and cases that should bring the book up to date. Check the date of the pocket part to see how current it is.

Case Reporters

From any of these sources you should be able to find at least a few cases related to your problem. Once you have these, look them up in the national series of *case reporters* published by West Publishing. This is a series of books containing all of the published cases in this country divided by region. The regions are as follows:

Atlantic (A.)	Pacific (P.)
California (Cal.Rptr.)	Southern (So.)
New York State (N.Y.S.)	Southeast (S.E.)
Northeast (N.E.)	Southwest (S.W.)
Northwest (N.W.)	

Your state might not be in the reporter you expect. For example, Kansas is in the Pacific Reporter, Michigan is in the Northwest Reporter and Vermont is in the Atlantic Reporter. (This is because at the time these books were started, Michigan was considered the northwest of the U.S. and Kansas was somewhere out near the Pacific.)

Case citation. A case citation has three parts: the volume, the series, and the page. Thus, 394 N.Y.S.2d 777 would be found in volume 394 of the New York Supplement 2d Series Reporters at page 777.

Headnotes. Once you have found a case similar to yours in one of these reporters, you should look at the beginning of the case for the *headnotes*. These are the summaries of the different holdings of the case. A case may have one or dozens of holdings. Some of the holdings may be directly related to the issue you are researching and others may have nothing to do with it.

Key numbers. Look for the holdings most closely related to your case and write down the *key numbers*. This is a system of categorizing cases by subject created and owned by the West Publishing Co. that publishes the reporters. By using these key numbers, you can locate other cases that have ruled on the same issues.

Digests

After you have the West key numbers of the issues you are researching, locate your state *digest*. This is a collection of all the head notes from all the cases in your state. (There are digests for every state except Delaware, Nevada and Utah.) By using the key numbers, you can find all of the other cases in your state on the subject.

NOTE: *If you are in Delaware, Nevada, or Utah, or if you want to check decisions from other states you can use the decennial digest. It is a digest of cases from all states published every ten years. In the interim, volumes are published every few months to bring it up to date.*

Shepard's Database

When you find a case that seems to cover exactly the topic you are interested in, see if any other case or legal article talked about it by *Shepardizing* it. This means you look it up in a database called *Shepards*. Shepards is available as a book and electronically. By looking up a case citation, you will get a list of everywhere that the cited case was mentioned.

USING THE INTERNET

The Internet provides a nearly infinite amount of free information. But unfortunately, much of it is worth what you pay for it. You can find a lot of hard law, statutes, and court cases, but not much legal analysis of specific issues that you might be interested in.

The best legal information on the Internet is the statutes and municipal ordinances. The statutes of all fifty states are available at no charge. There are several sites that link to the sites for the statutes of all fifty states. Here are a few:

www.law.cornell.edu

www.findlaw.com

www.prairienet.org

Unfortunately, some of the state statutes are very hard to search. You may find it easier to use the books of statutes at your local library. If you have an unusual word that applies to your problem, like a neighbors' *clothesline*, you may be able to find out if there is a law, quickly. But if you need to look up something like *noise*, you may get hundreds of references, most of which have no relation to what you are looking for. In such a case, using the index may be better than a computer search.

Some state statutes have poor indexes and the table of contents is the best place to start. From there you just need to page through the sections covering your subject. Another alternative is to use a fee-based legal research service such as Lexis, Lois or Westlaw. These are expensive to subscribe to, but some law libraries have them available at no charge.

When reading statutes, remember that many words have special legal meanings that may be different from the common meaning of the words. Also, statutes are sometimes interpreted by judges to mean something that is not clear from the words as they are actually written.

To better understand what a statute means you should check the *annotated statutes* that are available in most law libraries and some public libraries. Annotated statutes have a list of all the court cases, articles, and other interpretations listed after each law. Some have hundreds of cases interpreting their meaning and others have none. If you are in luck, there will be at least a few cases that help explain what your rights are under the statute.

State constitutions can be found through some of the same links as stated for the statutes listed earlier.

Municipal codes for many cities can be found at this website:
www.findlaw.com/11stategov/municipla.html

Recent case law is also available at no charge on the Internet. Some court systems have only posted their cases of the last few years. Others have begun posting prior years and become more complete each year. State court opinions can be found by going to:
www.law.cornell.edu/opinions.html#state

For some specialized topics, such as dealing with the government (discussed in Chapter 8), there are many sites. You can sometimes find these by using the Google search engine:
www.google.com

GLOSSARY

A

abatement. Stopping a problem on your own without confronting the person causing it.

abstract of title. A compilation of all legal documents affecting a piece of real estate.

actionable nuisance. An annoying situation that is serious enough to take to court.

adverse possession. Use of a piece of real estate for a long enough time to obtain ownership of it.

aesthetic zoning. Government controls that mandate the appearance of property.

annotated statutes. Compilation of laws that has applicable court cases listed after each statute.

arbitration. A disinterested third party, not part of the court system, decides a dispute.

assault. Putting a person in fear of being beaten.

B

battery. Causing contact with a person's body.

binding arbitration. A disinterested third party, not part of the court system, decides a dispute and all parties agree that the arbitrator's decision will be final.

C

Comprehensive Environmental Response, Compensation, and Liability Act (CERCLA). A federal law controlling cleanup of polluted property.

civil law. Laws governing relations between citizens.

code. A compilation of laws for a municipality or state.

commercial speech. The providing of information in order to sell a product or service.

common law. The legal rights found in court decisions.

compensatory damages. Money given to pay off actual monetary losses.

conditions. Rules for the use of real property.

condominium. A residential unit in a multiunit building that is typically owned by occupant instead of rented.

covenants. Agreements to use a piece of property in a certain way.

D

declaration of condominium. The legal document that spells out the rights of owners of condominium units.

deed. A legal document that transfers ownership of real property.

deed restrictions. Rules covering real property that pass from owner to owner by way of the deed.

due process. The right guaranteed by the U.S. Constitution to have a certain process followed before one's rights are taken by the government.

damages. Money paid to a party to make up for a wrongful act.

E

easement. The right to use the property owned by someone else.

eminent domain. The right a governmental body has to take ownership of private land and convert it to public use.

encroachment. Something that crosses a property boundary and trespasses on the next property.

equal protection. The right guaranteed by the U. S. Constitution to be treated equally to others similarly situated.

J

just compensation. Being paid a fair amount when the government takes private property.

L

laches. The loss of a legal right by failure to enforce it over a period of time.

libel. Publishing something false and harmful about a person.

lien. A claim against real property that is recognized by the law.

M

mediation. Working out a disagreement by having an independent party try to bring the parties to a compromise.

municipality. A local government jurisdiction.

N

necessary party. A person whose participation is required in a lawsuit in order to fairly adjudicate the issues.

negligence. Failure to use the proper amount of care in doing an act.

nuisance. Activity that annoys or disturbs neighbors.

O

ordinance. A law passed by a city, county or other local subdivision of the state.

P

party wall. A structure between two properties that is owned by both owners.

planned unit development. A community built according to a detailed plan.

prescriptive easement. An easement that is created by use over a long period of time.

privacy. The right to not have one's personal facts shared with others.

procedural due process. The right guaranteed by the U.S. Constitution that a fair procedure must be followed by the government before it can take a person's rights.

public nuisance. An activity that annoys or disturbs the public at large and not just immediate neighbors.

planned unit development (PUD). An area of land zoned for a community subdivision with flexible restrictions on property uses.

punitive damages. Monetary payment for a wrongful act that is above the amounts needed for compensation and intended to punish the wrongdoer.

R

restrictions. Controls put on the use of land.

restrictive covenants. Rules that control actions on real property.

S

slander. Saying something false and harmful about a person.

spite fence. A fence or other structure put up with the main purpose of annoying a neighbor.

spot zoning. Zoning one piece of property different from the surrounding properties, inconsistent with the overall plan.

statute of limitations. A law stating how long a period of time a person has after an event in which to file a lawsuit concerning the event.

statute. A law passed by a state.

substantive due process. The right guaranteed by the U.S. Constitution that the government cannot take away a person's rights without clear justification.

T

trespass. Unlawfully entering on or over another's property.

U

unconstitutional. A law that violated a right guaranteed by a state or federal constitution.

Z

zoning. Laws restricting the use of real property.

–Checklist–
HOW TO SOLVE A NEIGHBOR PROBLEM

☐ Have you approached the person causing the problem?

☐ Can you solve it yourself?

☐ Would the perpetrator agree to mediation or arbitration?

☐ Do any covenants or restrictions help you?

☐ Is there a homeowners' association or condo board?

☐ Is there a law that supports your position?

☐ Will the police help?

☐ Is there another municipal office that can help?

☐ Have you consulted with an attorney?

☐ Is it worth taking to court?

☐ Do you have enough legal research to back up your case?

☐ Does the perpetrator have a good defense?

☐ Are there other neighbors who agree with you?

☐ Do you have enough evidence?

☐ Is it worth appealing?

☐ Would it be easier and/or cheaper to move?

INDEX

138, 142, 149, 151, 152, 153,
161, 166, 167, 168
abandon, 20
damage, 110
devalue, 2, 18
diminished value, 136, 151
disposition of, 23
dominant, 26
estimated value, 132
legal description, 4, 6
legal rights, 24
private, 24, 133
rental, 173
slum, 132
undervalued, 131
value, 95, 118, 131, 151, 161
property law, 48
property line, 30, 32, 83, 87, 92,
95, 98

Q

quarantine statutes, 58
quarry, 53
questions of fact, 178, 179
questions of law, 178
quit claim, 84

R

racetrack, 109
racial discrimination, 41
radio, 111
radioactivity, 101
radiological hazards, 119
railroad, 12, 24, 64, 81, 170
rain, 32, 50, 101, 104
ranches, 91
real estate, 31
real estate agent, 3
real estate contract, 3
real estate law, 5
recorder's office, 5
recovery, 53
referendums, 130
regulations, 5

regulatory code, 45
release, 35
remedy, 5, 6, 15, 29, 45, 47, 58, 69,
72, 96, 112, 119, 137, 147
rendering plant, 75
rented, 5, 7, 20, 25, 39, 57, 78,
105, 147, 161, 164
renter, 1, 162
residential area, 55, 171
residential zone, 54, 146
residents, 5, 25, 40, 54, 64, 67, 72,
114, 115, 117, 137, 139, 141,
148, 170, 171
resolution, 84
fair, 84
Resource Conservation and
Recovery Act, 112
responsibility, 12
Restatement of Torts, 160
Restatement Rule, 96, 97
restraint on alienation, 38
restriction laws, 53
restrictions, 2, 3, 4, 6, 7, 12, 28, 29,
37–40, 174
restrictive covenants, 2, 30, 37
retaining wall, 49, 51
rezoning, 41
right by prescription, 31
right of access, 7
right of first refusal, 38
right to farm laws, 170
right to just compensation for
property taken by the government, 16, 17
riot, 16
riparian rights, 102
river, 101, 102
Rivers and Harbors Act, 112
roof, 30, 32
roots, 96, 98, 99, 122
runway, 140
rural areas, 91, 93, 99, 100